P9-DZX-979

the quest for
$ecurity

THE CENTER FOR THE STUDY OF
THE RECENT HISTORY OF THE UNITED STATES

A cooperative undertaking involving
The State Historical Society of Iowa
The Herbert Hoover Presidential Library
and
The University of Iowa

The QUEST for $ECURITY

Papers on the Origins and the Future of the American Social Insurance System

Edited by John N. Schacht

The Center for the
Study of the Recent History of the United States

© Copyright 1982 by the Center for the Study
of the Recent History of the United States
All rights reserved
Printed in the United States of America

Library of Congress Cataloging in Publication Data

Main entry under title:

The Quest for security.

Proceedings of a conference held October 7, 1981
in Iowa City, sponsored by the Center for the Study of
the Recent History of the United States.
Includes bibliographical references.
1. Social security—United States—History—
Congresses. I. Schacht, John N., 1943—   . II. Center
for the Study of the Recent History of the United
States (Iowa City, Iowa)
HD7125.Q47   1982   368.4'3'00973   82-17549
ISBN 0-87414-026-9

Contents

194761

Foreword

MOST AMERICANS have come to consider social security to be a purely domestic concern limited to the United States. Yet students of international history have realized that when the social security program was enacted under the aegis of the New Deal in 1935, the United States was among the last of the industrial countries to provide workers with a compulsory program of social insurance. So widespread had popular acceptance of the concept become by 1941 that, following the onset of the Second World War, President Franklin Roosevelt and Britain's Prime Minister Winston Churchill included social security as the fifth provision of the Atlantic Charter, setting forth their common aspirations for the postwar world. Less than a month after Pearl Harbor, on January 1, 1942, governments at war with the Axis signed the Declaration of the United Nations, in which the signatories explicitly subscribed to the Atlantic Charter. This process of universalizing the concept of social security is a matter that should be borne in mind by Americans as they now contemplate the present and future status of social security in the United States.

The five papers that follow were first presented at a conference entitled "The Quest for Security," held in Iowa City on October 7, 1981, under the sponsorship of the Center for the Study of the Recent History of the United States. The first four papers, delivered to an afternoon audience consisting mostly of historians, were presented in conference format under the broad heading "Origins of the American Social Insurance System." They seek to explain the historical circumstances that led Americans of various political persuasions to favor social insurance programs during the years between the two world wars. Initially, social security legislation was a modest proposal designed to protect only certain categories of workers. Since 1935, however, it has been gradually extended to provide coverage to virtually all salaried employees and wage earners in the private sector, to some categories of the self-employed, and to many state and local government employees across the country. Yet, as we move into the last two decades of the twentieth century, social security in the United States is encountering fiscal crisis. Persons becoming eligible for retirement benefits are wondering whether the system will weather the crisis and provide the promised benefits toward which they and their employers have contributed over many years—and upon which they have based their plans and expectations. Younger Americans are concerned about whether they will have to contribute ever higher premiums to a social security system that may not exist at the time retirement beckons. There are some Americans who now favor a sharp curtailment, a redirection, even an entire reconsideration of social security. The fifth paper in the volume is addressed in particular to those pressing issues and concerns. Entitled "Social Security: New Directions," it was initially presented to an evening audience enlarged by the presence of many persons outside the historical profession. All five papers, dealing with social insurance past and present, deserve thoughtful consideration as the national debate continues.

The Center for the Study of the Recent History of the United States is a consortium whose participating institutions are the State Historical Society of Iowa, the Herbert Hoover Presidential Library, and the University of Iowa. I am pleased to acknowledge the splendid support and cooperation of the institutional representatives whose services have contributed to both past and ongoing projects of the Center: Dale M. Bentz, University Librarian; Robert A. McCown, Manuscripts Librarian in the University Libraries; Thomas T. Thalken, Director of the Herbert Hoover Presidential Library; R. Lawrence Angove, Executive Secretary of the Hoover Presidential Library Association; Loren N. Horton, Acting Director of the State Historical Society of Iowa; and Ellis W. Hawley, Professor of History at the University of Iowa. The Center owes a special debt to Leslie W. Dunlap, Dean Emeritus of Library Administration at the University of Iowa, who until his retirement in December, 1981, served as chairman of the Advisory Committee. I want to thank Peter T. Harstad, who was until May, 1981, Director of the State Historical Society of Iowa and who served as a charter member of the Center's Advisory Committee, and John N. Schacht, of the University Libraries, who prepared these and earlier conference papers for publication. On behalf of the Center, I want to express our gratitude to the University of Iowa Foundation, the Proctor and Gamble Fund, and Mr. and Mrs. Clem T. Hanson, of Moline, Illinois, whose financial support has been a mainstay for these conferences and the publication of the conferences' proceedings.

June 15, 1982   Lawrence E. Gelfand
                                    Professor of History, The University
                                    of Iowa
                                    Chairman of the Advisory Committee

Social Reform, Social Work, and Social Security: A Subject Revisited

Clarke A. Chambers

MANY HEADLINES since January 20 of this year have heralded the demise of the New Deal; finally, the news stories proclaim, after a half century in which measures inaugurated during the Great Depression had been extended and expanded by a succession of presidents (four Democrats and three Republicans), these programs were to be reversed and the political coalition forged by Franklin Roosevelt was to be broken. Fifty years, in American politics, seems a near eternity. Five decades carried the nation from Jefferson to Lincoln, from Grant to Wilson, from FDR to Reagan.

The times do change, events do move, mandates are fulfilled and relapse, and recent months provide ample evidence of drastic change. Budgets have been slashed (in all areas save the military and subsidies to tobacco growers). Regressive tax strategies have replaced progressive. The conservation of natural resources has fallen to ideologies, presumably rooted in Old Testament admonitions that declare the earth to be under the dominion of the sons of Adam, and has been given over to hastening exploitation. The regulatory powers of federal government have been weakened (although the grip of the Federal Reserve on money supply and interest rates appears tighter than ever). Knights on white chargers, their shields blazoned "Supply Side Economics," have bested economists mounted on tired Keynesian nags (although it may be fair to say that for most citizens both economic theories have remained more in the realm of Merlin than of Arthur). Of course, there had been slippage long before the knights from southern California drove out the lords from southern Georgia. Many regulatory commissions had come under control of the very interests that were to be policed, presumably in the public interest. Nixon, Ford, and Carter had begun to relax the federal authority in many spheres. And the Tennessee Valley Authority, once hailed as a giant step toward benign and democratic socialism, came, as

Clarke A. Chambers is Professor of History and Director of the Social Welfare History Archives Center, University of Minnesota.

1

early as the 1950s, to be the chief polluter of the natural and social environment in that great valley.

As for social security, it stands for the moment vulnerable to modifications that threaten to whittle away some of its benefits and in jeopardy of insolvency unless more drastic tactics are employed—although David Stockman's prophecies of bankruptcy reflect the hyperbolic rhetorical style which marks his demeanor generally. Yet of all New Deal programs, it seems the most secure. Rulings defining the financial responsibility of stepparents will reduce levels of benefits to some families on Aid to Families with Dependent Children, but not many. The minimum payment may be reduced, thus pushing many recipients off social security and onto welfare. The age of elibigility for retirement benefits may edge upward, but gradually, one imagines, and without repeal of the basic right to benefits. Unemployment insurance, as vital to sustained economic growth as to family security, remains in place.

That had been Roosevelt's explicit design in 1935, when the president—strongly backed by his secretary of labor, Frances Perkins, and by E. E. Witte, chief of staff of the Committee on Economic Security (the mother and father, respectively, of social security)—insisted on the establishment of a system of social insurance that would be national, compulsory, and contributory, with recipients entitled to benefits as a right, not as a gratuity. FDR, rejoicing in his 1935 victory, put it bluntly: it was "politics all the way through. We put the payroll deductions there so as to give the contributors a legal, moral and political right to collect their pensions and their unemployment benefits. With those taxes in there, no damn politician can ever scrap my social security program."[1] And we have Frances Perkins's assurance that to FDR the act was the "cornerstone of his adminstration," and from its passage he gained greater satisfaction than from any other domestic accomplishment.[2]

Early general historical accounts of the New Deal each devoted some pages to the origins and shaping of social security, and various memoirs and reminiscences, most notably Perkins's *The Roosevelt I Knew* (1946), rendered various significant details. But it was not until the 1960s, some thirty years after the event and in the context of the War on Poverty, that professional historians began to publish extended analyses focused on the processes by which social insurance was introduced in this country, many decades after other Western industrial countries had inaugurated comprehensive national systems. Over the past fifteen years the historical literature has become very rich indeed, and 1981 provides an appropriate moment for a review, both historical and historiographic.

You will understand if I begin with a few personal, subjective comments on my own *Seedtime of Reform,* not only because it was one of the first monographs (researched and written 1960-62, published in 1963) dealing with the origins of social insurance as one of many related reforms in the arenas of welfare and labor legislation, but also because it happens that I know that study more intimately than others.[3] At the outset let me explain that the title was not intended to portray the era, 1918-1933, as a time hospitable to varied social justice movements that had originated in the era we used to know as progressive until Gabriel Kolko came along to advise us otherwise. That title, I hasten to add, was a hurried second choice. The title I had originally proposed had been drawn from a poignant statement by Grace Abbott, toward the end of her remarkable career, to the effect that the struggle for humane reform and social justice, whatever its rewards, was *uphill all the way.* Unhappily, my publisher discovered that copyright to that title was already occupied by a how-to book on mountaineering and upcountry camping and could not be used!

My original intent was direct and clear: to trace the continuity of the social reform impulse in the years between the First World War and the coming of the New Deal. My beginning hunch was not only simple but in its way simple-minded—if historians all but universally portrayed the twenties as a decade of reaction and normalcy, a jazz age, an age of wonderful nonsense, those designations, I suspected, must be partial and flawed. What did the social justice wing of progressivism do when times were inhospitable to the causes it had pursued? What careers did politicians and public servants who came to power in the 1930s follow in their formative, apprentice years? The evidence led me to a consideration of myriad voluntary associations that continued to agitate for public housing, labor legislation, adequate public assistance for needy families and dependent children, federal grants for maternal and child health (the Sheppard-Towner program, enacted in 1921 and in force until 1929), work relief as preferred to a cash dole in hard times, old age pensions, and unemployment insurance. The evidence led me also to the role played by an activist minority of social work leaders, many of them women, who continued to press the human service professions to recognize their responsibility to be active in the formulation of public policy in the fields of health and welfare. Several chapters focused on the search for effective and refined means of providing security against the hazards of dependent old age and unemployment, and to provide constructive income programs that would provide financial stability for families rendered insecure by injury, sickness, or death of the chief wage-earner, or else broken by desertion or divorce.

Welfare measures of the New Deal proved quickly effective, I concluded, not only because persisting hard times created a climate favorable to government action, not only because the New Deal was ably led by imaginative and canny politicians, but also because "professional social work evidenced a persisting concern for the general welfare of society as for the health of the individual client," and because reform and welfare leaders "kept alive the tradition of humane liberalism in the years of normalcy."[4] The detailed analysis cut off in 1933 and did not trace the implementation of these policies, except in passing, during the New Deal years. The book focused on the planting of the seeds for reform, not on the harvest.

Reviewing that work this summer in preparation for this conference, I was struck by two considerations: (1) much of the primary data—especially evidence that documents the role of professional welfare associations and agencies—was unavailable to scholars in the early sixties; and (2) the great body of secondary work that focused on the enactment of social security in 1935 had not yet been published. Detailed inside accounts by active participants in the events of 1934-35, including those by E. E. Witte, Arthur Altmeyer, J. Douglas Brown, and Charles McKinley and Robert Frase, were published in the 1962-72 period. Secondary works bearing on social insurance movements and policies by Roy Lubove, Daniel Nelson, and Hace Tishler appeared during 1968-71, and as recently as 1980 there appeared a major revisionist interpretation by Edward D. Berkowitz and Kim McQuaid.[5] It was not until 1964, with the establishment of the Social Welfare History Archives at the University of Minnesota, that scholars have had full access to the records of national social work associations that played a major role in the shaping of public policy during the twentieth century.[6]

For our purposes at this conference, the secondary literature can be reviewed by looking first at those special studies that surveyed the movements for social insurance which culminated in the writing and passage of the 1935 Social Security Act. Another set of studies has provided detailed, sometimes day-by-day, narratives of the work of the Committee on Economic Security, 1934-35, and the complicated process by which its report was enacted into law; these studies often include commentary on the impact of the Townsend old age pension movement upon public opinion and legislative response. Finally, I wish to review some of the data contained in the primary historical records now available at the Minnesota Center, insofar as they throw additional light on the contribution of professional social work during the early years of the Great Depression.

Roy Lubove's solid account of *The Struggle for Social Security, 1900-1935* (1968) is probably the book most often cited in other historical works dealing with this subject. Focusing on early movements for workmen's compensation, health insurance, mothers' pensions, old age pensions, and unemployment insurance, Lubove correctly attributes the relative weakness of these crusades to the persisting power of the American ideology of voluntarism. Any system of compusory insurance, he writes, "seemed hostile to American traditions. Critics of social insurance interpreted the real issue as paternalism and statism versus personal liberty and voluntarism."[7] Although proponents of social insurance argued that voluntary systems could never provide for those workers and families that were most vulnerable to the insecurities of employment and income that marked modern industrialism, the public generally remained apathetic while enlightened industrial leaders proposed stabilization through welfare capitalism, and organized labor accepted Samual Gompers's conviction that the initiation of governmental insurance would subvert free trade unionism. Yet corporate pension schemes, originating in employers' desire to reduce labor turnover and promote employee loyalty, in fact provided instruments for disciplining the work force; irresponsibly financed, they covered only a small fraction of the work force by 1930. Experiments in several states with old age pensions were weakened by county option provisions, by inadequate financing, and by negligible benefits.

The main body of Lubove's study is devoted to the efforts of a small band of insurance pioneers: John R. Commons, Richard T. Ely, John B. Andrews (a director of the American Association for Labor Legislation from its founding in 1906), Isaac Rubinow and Abraham Epstein (both of whom worked from European models), William Leiserson, and Don D. Lescohier (who borrowed heavily from Beveridge and the English precedent). Although their labors won meager success during these years, and many of them were not consulted when the Social Security Act was being drafted, their efforts helped inform influential economic and political leaders and helped lay the ground for the inauguration of social insurance in the 1930s.

In *Self-Reliance and Social Security, 1870-1917* (1971) Hace Tishler concerns himself more with ideological components of social insurance movements than with the details of early programs, although his account includes extended commentary on workmen's compensation, widows' pensions, and health insurance. Arguing, incorrectly I believe, that the movements lay dormant until the Great Depression forced a revived interest in security, he insists that the major contribution of reformers in the earlier period was to redefine and overcome the long-held American ethic of "thrift, industriousness and self-reliance" and the notion that individuals must provide for themselves.[8]   Such early pioneers as Rubinow, Commons, Ely, Edward Devine and others, moved by the disharmony and class conflict that seemed to mark industrial relations in their generation, established the point that poverty was rooted in unemployment, sickness, and old age—causes of need over which workmen and their families had no control. The logic of events compelled society first to recognize and then to assume its ultimate responsibility for providing security for its citizenry. The redefinition of self-reliance arose not only from social justice progressives but from corporate architects of welfare capitalism as well, whose ethic of social efficiency and scientific management— expressed most notably in the support which leaders of large corporations gave to workmen's compensation—helped lead business and government to conclude that security was not the antithesis but the salvation of self-reliance in modern circumstances.

It was left to Daniel Nelson's compact and intricate study of *Unemployment Insurance* (1969) to set forth the complex and often conflicting strands of theory and program that characterized the debate in the twenty years leading to the 1935 enactment, a debate that engaged only a handful of specialists, for there was little popular interest until persisting mass unemployment forced a resolution in the thirties. Nelson demonstrates that at least until 1931-32 the best of the dialogue rested with scholars and publicists connected with the "Wisconsin School" (Commons, Andrews, Paul Raushenbush, and Elizabeth Brandeis), which placed chief emphasis on the initiation of industrial reserves as an incentive to corporations to stabilize employment; in that regard their efforts ran parallel to those of enlightened employers who resisted the inauguration of government programs. Opposed to this strategy was a coalition composed of "intellectuals, social workers, clergymen, and reformers" who proposed a "comprehensive national system of social insurance" on the European model, whose spokesmen included Epstein, Rubinow, and Paul Douglas.[9]

When the contest moved to the states in the early years of the depression (Nelson's survey includes extended sections on legislative struggles in Wisconsin, Massachusetts, New York, and Ohio), the weight shifted gradually toward guaranteed benefits for workers and away from stabilization, although even under conditions of deepening economic crisis, action continued to be frustrated by the inarticulateness of the unemployed, the passivity of organized labor, the deeply-rooted public skepticism of anything smacking of the European dole, and dissension among diverse insurance factions. In such a context it was possible for Roosevelt and Perkins, worried about the potential impact of the Townsend movement, to assume command and to shape a bill that would build a centrist consensus in favor of the social insurance principle. The act that finally emerged was a bundle of compromises. It disappointed many connected with the Wisconsin School (although two of its chief authors, Witte and Altmeyer, both came out of the Wisconsin experience); it provoked the criticism or outright opposition of many on the liberal left. But it was a safe bill and it worked from the legislative standpoint; it proved to be constitutional; and it did in fact build a firm foundation upon which a more elaborate and comprehensive system would be erected over time. One is led to the conclusion that although the particulars of the act did not fulfill the expectations of the founders of the social insurance movement, the generation-long agitation served to inform the perceptions of persons who would become forces for pragmatic action in 1935.

Most recently there has come a revisionist interpretation of the roots of social insurance from Edward D. Berkowitz and Kim McQuaid, who argue that it is to a body of businessmen and conservative public officials that social insurance owes its primary debt, men such as Edward Filene, Henry Dennison, Gerard Swope, Owen Young, Marion Folsom, Walter Teagle, and Herbert Hoover, whose social philosophy placed primary emphasis on the bureaucratic/business values of efficiency, coordination, rationalization, cost-effectiveness, stabilization of production, and regularization of employment.[10] Their argument, though it employs a different

BRIDWELL LIBRARY
SOUTHERN METHODIST UNIVERSITY
DALLAS, TEXAS 75275

vantage point and evaluation, supports in important ways the "conservative"-roots-of-reform hypothesis elaborated by Gabriel Kolko and James Weinstein.[11] Berkowitz and McQuaid propose that corporate leaders, especially in "technology-intensive, multi-product industries," had an interest in the elaboration of industrial and governmental strategies aimed at stabilizing the economy and thus quieting industrial unrest. They successfully demonstrate the influence of corporate leaders in the reduction of labor turnover, in promoting industrial safety and systems of compensation, in the enforcement of fair labor codes through trade associations and subsequently through the NRA, and in initiating an ideology of social engineering and corporate responsibility. But they provide a less persuasive case in establishing a clear and positive connection between these efforts and the emergence of social insurance as a chief component of a welfare state during the New Deal. It is true, as they argue, that the creators of the Social Security Act did indeed consult with such welfare capitalists as Swope, Young, and Teagle, and that the legislative program included a joint-contributory tactic for gathering funds for old age insurance, benefit levels based on earnings, and the principle of funded reserves without contributions from general tax revenues— all reflective of the experience and point of view of welfare capitalists.[12] Scholars of social insurance will welcome these additional and corrective data, but the preponderance of evidence demonstrates that other persons and forces played roles more important.[13]

When it comes to detailed examination of the concrete events of 1934-35, we must turn to another set of books, most significantly to accounts provided by the actors themselves (Perkins, Witte, Altmeyer, and McKinley and Frase), to notable biographies of Perkins and Witte, to specialized monographs that deal with aging and old age movements, and to general secondary works on the New Deal.[14]

From these works there emerge a number of conclusions that seem to confirm the contention that the publicity given to social insurance by social reformers provided experience and information that proved crucial in the enactment of a social security system, even though there was little agreement on particulars among the diverse factions that composed that coalition. Introduced as a state senator to the insecurities that pervaded life and labor in an industrial society, Franklin Roosevelt continued to be influenced by associates that numbered Perkins, Hopkins, Robert Wagner, Molly Dewson, and Lillian Wald, all of whom took advanced posi-

BRIDWELL LIBRARY
SOUTHERN METHODIST UNIVERSITY
DALLAS, TEXAS 75275

tions on welfare and labor legislation during the 1920s and became prime movers in the 1930s. Spurred on by Perkins, Roosevelt as governor of New York began to master the complex components of social insurance, and by 1931 he had publicly endorsed its principles. As president, with the desperate economic emergency of 1933-34 addressed if not overcome, he gave top priority to the long-range issue of social insurance and assigned Perkins, in June, 1934, to chair a cabinet committee to prepare legislation on economic security. That committee—the Committee on Economic Security (CES)—in turn called on Witte, an experienced Wisconsin public official and a person committed to social insurance but unaligned with any single faction, to serve as executive director. In weeks a staff of experts had been assembled, all of them specialists in one phase or another of security issues: Altmeyer to chair the Technical Board, Bryce Stewart to guide unemployment insurance, Barbara Armstrong and J. Douglas Brown to work on old age provisions, Katharine Lenroot and Martha B. Eliot of the Children's Bureau to advise on aid to dependent children and on child and maternal health, and a host of others of like training and disposition.

The appointment of an Advisory Council on Economic Security, chaired by Frank P. Graham of the University of North Carolina, proved less expedient. Originally conceived to be a small committee of representative citizens whose authority, it was hoped, would help build broad public support for whatever comprehensive system emerged, the membership was gradually enlarged to a point where it was unable to advise effectively. Even though such figures as Andrews, Epstein, Douglas, and Rubinow were excluded from the Council—this in the expectation (or prayer) that in their absence the level of disagreement could be contained—the deliberations of the group proved divisive on a number of particulars, a development that provided some embarrassment later, when the bill came before Congress. The charge to the Advisory Council had never been made clear; it had too little time to consider in depth the awesomely complex actuarial and legal issues that the staff itself found difficult to resolve. But events were moving quickly, and the CES paid little attention to its recommendations in any case. For the historian nearly a half-century later, the episode can be seen as an unhappy but finally not serious interruption in the process of forming an acceptable bill; it can be read also as evidence of the penchant of some social reformers to persevere in argumentation when the time had come for action. The writing of a comprehensive bill that would likely be constitutional and that would win favorable congressional action called for compromise and reconciliation—talents that Witte enjoyed in abundance.

In assessing the motives and forces that led to social security, historians have examined the influence of the Townsend old age pension movement that was just beginning to gather strength in 1934. There is no question that the administration's determination to act preceded the emergence of the Townsendites, although politicians of all persuasions, looking forward to November, 1934, and beyond that to 1936, were made uneasy by the rise of popular protest movements whose leaders—Father Coughlin, Huey Long, Dr. Francis Townsend—could not be contained within the two-party system. Given widespread disaffection and the persistence of hard times, anything could happen; and this volatility surely provoked FDR to be nimble and quick. The CES labored under daily pressure to prepare a bill for congressional attention early in 1935. Financial crisis had bankrupted large numbers of corporate and trade union pension programs; some states had begun to explore old age and unemployment insurance schemes, though local and state governments clearly lacked the financial resources; only the federal government was equal to the task. Unless constructive measures were enacted, and quickly, the nation might be seduced by unsound panaceas.

Pressure on the CES mounted. Fifteen hundred letters a day, most of them from the Townsend folk, reached Witte's office during the fall of 1934; and Perkins, speaking before diverse audiences across the country, reported growing sentiment for action on unemployment and old age insecurity. When the bill was before Congress in the winter of 1935, the testimony of Townsend and his associates received the widest press coverage, but the net effect of their witness was probably to reveal the fiscal absurdity of the Townsend proposal and thereby to draw support to the administration program, inadequate and flawed as it appeared to many of its friendly critics. Writing in 1962, Perkins recalled that the Townsend movement "both drove us and confused the issue. Without the Townsend plan, it is possible that the old-age insurance system would not have received the attention which it did at the hands of Congress."[15] The judgment of the Townsend movement's chief historian, Abraham Holtzman, tends to confirm the assessment of Perkins, Witte, and Altmeyer: it "compelled an immediate consideration of old-age security legislation"; it "crystallized tremen-

dous popular sentiment in favor of old-age security"; and it "weakened conservative opposition" to the Social Security Act itself.[16]

But it was not until the 1960s that a successful organization of
old age lobbies came to enjoy influence on national policy. The
initiative for old age insurance and assistance in 1935 derived not
from popular movements but from a relatively small coalition of
citizens. The same is true for unemployment insurance. Until
1932 organized labor had been hostile or at best apathetic toward
it, and union leadership, having set other legislative priorities,
played only a modest supporting role in 1935.

The intent of this essay does not call for a careful analysis of
the act itself, but several observations may be pertinent. Political
strategy called for a single comprehensive bill with several titles,
so that less popular sections would be carried by the more appeal-
ing. The bulk of congressional interest focused on old age insurance and assistance, although the CES and its Technical Board
had spent far more time and energy on the unemployment insurance titles. Federal assumption of a substantial part of the financial responsibility for dependent children slipped by with little
debate; while the benefits remained niggardly and the rates were
effectively to be set by the states, the more punitive aspects of
mothers' pensions, with their "morals" tests, were relaxed. Consideration of health insurance, in the face of vehement opposition
from the medical profession, was indefinitely postponed. Federal
aid to programs for maternal and infant health, a favored program of social workers and women's groups earlier embodied in
the Sheppard-Towner Act, was easily revived.

Although social democratic liberals and radicals among the social reform groups favored the financing of social security out of
general tax revenues (a device they hoped would spur redistribution of income), Roosevelt and his associates insisted on a contributory system, even though it meant regressive and deflationary
taxation, arguing (soundly, as events turned out) that only if recipients—the unemployed and the aged—had legal entitlement to
benefits as a right would social security achieve permanent status.
Those who contributed to reserves for unemployment and old age
would have a stake in the system; legal entitlement presumably
would foster dignity in recipients, whereas gratuitous payments,
which could be raised or lowered or even discontinued at the
whim of Congress, lowered morale and rendered the system vulnerable to sudden shifts in public policy. As the president insisted,
unemployment compensation was not to be a "charity"; it was to

be financed by "contributions not taxes."[17] On the other hand, the categories of workers covered were relatively limited. Farm laborers, domestic servants, and government employees, for example, were exempted from the original act. The use of dollar-matching for all titles except those covering old age made more likely the ultimate constitutionality of the act.

In short, the Social Security Act was a jumble of separate measures, eclectic in social theory, which mixed contributory insurance with programs of categorical aid financed from general revenues. It promised security down the line for millions of citizens, without the introduction of any fundamental changes in the economic or social order. To Frank Bruno, an acerbic social work educator, it was a "miscellaneous" act, a "measure to furnish such means of security as do not arouse serious opposition."[18] Yet, over time, by amendment, the system became the foundation of a largely effective security program.

Addressing the National Conference of Social Work in May, 1934, Harry Hopkins reviewed the issues that confronted the nation: poverty, old age pensions, widows' pensions, unemployment insurance, public works, work relief, and health insurance. "No group of people in America," he assured his sympathetic audience, "have been so impatient in our treatment of poverty as have the social workers." They "have carried this gospel" of preventive and constructive measures "from one end of the country to the other for the past fifty years."[19] The historical evidence, it seems to me after a survey of the literature, suggests that Hopkins's assessment, however much it may have been designed to flatter his audience and inspire it to higher levels of political involvement, has proved basically sound. Even if one adds a few powerful corporate leaders who had evolved a philosophy and programs of welfare capitalism, and even if one adds a mere handful of labor leaders who had come around to an acceptance of social insurance during the early 1930s (John L. Lewis, Philip Murray, and Sidney Hillman with enthusiasm, William Green with marked reluctance), it still remains the case that a coalition of social reformers and social workers, moved by a vision of social justice and social democracy that in no way challenged traditional economic structures or political processes, composed a cadre of concern that played the largest role in preparing the way for a broad acceptance of a social insurance strategy, in designing the program itself, and in carrying it through to enactment.

It also took a depression, of course, and a president of consummate political skill, who assigned the task of implementation to a team of politicians and expert technicians who shared both his pragmatism and his commitment to economic security. The modesty of the original act—its niggardliness, its deficiencies, which social workers and social reformers were the first to denounce and seek to remedy—in no way disturbs that historical conclusion.

Primary historical records that have become available for scholarly research since the mid-sixties corroborate the importance of the efforts of human service practitioners and the associations through which they worked in the shaping of opinion and policy on a wide range of public issues related to social insurance.[20] The American Association of Social Workers, for example, established in October, 1931, a Steering Committee on Federal Action on Unemployment (renamed the Committee on Federal Action on Social Welfare in December, 1933), which studied, reported, endorsed, and worked for such policies as the federal assumption of responsibility for relief, work relief, public works, fair labor standards, and social insurance. Leaders of this committee regularly corresponded and conferred with such congressional leaders as Senators Wagner, Costigan, Harrison, La Follette, and Norris and Representatives Lewis and Dole—all of whom played crucial roles in social legislation, 1931 to 1935—and with Perkins, Hopkins, Raymond Moley, and FDR. On the social work side, the most active leaders included Walter West, Linton Swift, David Holbrook, Mary Van Kleeck, William Hodson, Joanna Colcord, Harry Lurie, and Isaac Rubinow. Minutes and proceedings of the National Social Work Council, an umbrella association with membership from some fifty voluntary welfare societies, document the same range of concerns and opinion. During the crucial months of 1934-35 when the social insurance program was being developed, the Council's deliberations were informed by communications with Barbara Armstrong, E. E. Witte, Ewan Clague, Josephine Roche, Katherine Lenroot, Martha Eliot, and Arthur Altmeyer. Nor can one ignore the contribution of the *Survey* and *Survey Graphic* in educating elites in social work, law, public administration, health, education, and politics on these complex issues.[21]

Harry Hopkins, in 1934, praised social workers for having been in the vanguard of progressive social legislation. Addressing the same sort of constituency the following year, Harry Lurie—by 1935 a forceful leader of the radical rank-and-file movement— complained that social work, in his lifetime, had been largely "remedial," and that social workers had not, on the whole, "played a conspicuous part in the development of a consistent or comprehensive program of social legislation." The profession, he continued, had generally "tied up with the reactionary rather than with the advancing forces of social change." Far more to be credited, he felt, were the commanding efforts of such voluntary reform groups as the Child Labor Committee, the American Association for Social Security, and the American Association for Labor Legislation.[22] Lurie's commentary can be appreciated as arising out of disappointment with the failure of social insurance and related New Deal measures to address what he and his associates saw as a need for a drastic reordering of society along social democratic lines, and out of disenchantment with the moderation of most people engaged in human services, who were willing to accept (and even endorse) Roosevelt's piecemeal programs. Even persons closer to the center—Paul Kellogg, Helen Hall, John Andrews, Isaac Rubinow—were critical in 1935 of what they saw as tentative and excessively prudent provisions of the Social Security Act, and although they finally supported it as perhaps the best that could be achieved at that moment, given the president's anxieties regarding constitutional and legislative feasibility, they soon began to work for its amendment.

Theron Schlabach concludes in his masterful biography of E. E. Witte that advocates of social insurance in 1934, at the time of the appointment of the Committee on Economic Security, were "frustrated, divided, and quarrelsome."[23] His is probably an accurate assessment, as applicable for 1935 as for 1934. So it was Witte's task to find common ground for a bill behind which the administration could build an effective majority. In that campaign Witte and the administration succeeded, in substantial part owing to the coalition of social reformers and experts in economics and social work whose efforts, over a generation, had prepared the way.

NOTES

1   Roosevelt quoted in Charles McKinley and Robert W. Frase, *Launching Social Security: A Capture-and-Record Account, 1935-1937* (Madison, 1970), 17.

2   Frances Perkins, *The Roosevelt I Knew* (New York, 1946), 301.

3   Clarke A. Chambers, *Seedtime of Reform: Social Service and Social Action, 1918-1933* (Minneapolis, 1963).

4   *Ibid.*, 263, 267.

5   Edwin E. Witte, *The Development of the Social Security Act: A Memorandum on the History of the Committee on Economic Security and Drafting and Legislative*

History of the Social Security Act (Madison, 1962; composed in the mid-1930s); Arthur Altmeyer, *The Formative Years of Social Security* (Madison, 1968); McKinley and Frase, *Launching Social Security;* J. Douglas Brown, *An American Philosophy of Social Security: Evolution and Issues* (Princeton, 1972); Roy Lubove, *The Struggle for Social Security, 1900-1935* (Cambridge, Mass., 1968); Daniel Nelson, *Unemployment Insurance: The American Experience, 1915-1935* (Madison, 1969); Hace Tishler, *Self-Reliance and Social Security, 1870-1917* (New York, 1971); Edward D. Berkowitz and Kim McQuaid, *Creating the Welfare State: The Political Economy of Twentieth-Century Reform* (New York, 1980).

6   An inventory of these collections may be obtained by writing David Klaassen, Curator of the Social Welfare History Archives Center, University of Minnesota, Minneapolis, MN 55455, and enclosing one dollar to cover expenses.

7   Lubove, *The Struggle for Social Security,* 5.

8   Tishler, *Self-Reliance and Social Security,* ix.

9   Nelson, *Unemployment Insurance,* 9.

10   Berkowitz and McQuaid, *Creating the Welfare State.* The hypothesis was first set forth in their "Businessman and Bureaucrat: The Evolution of the American Social Welfare System, 1900-1940," *Journal of Economic History,* 38 (March, 1978), 120-42.

11   Gabriel Kolko, *The Triumph of Conservatism: A Reinterpretation of American History, 1900-1916* (New York, 1963); James Weinstein, *The Corporate Ideal in the Liberal State, 1900-1918* (Boston, 1968). In *The Social Responsibilities of Business: Company and Community, 1900-1960* (Cleveland, 1970), Morrell Heald traces the growth of philanthropic thought and policies of business leaders. This book is a useful study of ideology and practice, which does not, however, specifically include a discussion of the interest of welfare capitalism in social insurance.

12   J. Douglas Brown, a member of the technical staff, 1934-35, recalls that in December, 1934, the support of Teagle, Swope, and Folsom for a broad, national program of old age insurance carried authority with many conservatives and helped to offset the reservations of Secretary of the Treasury Henry Morgenthau, Jr. *An American Philosophy of Social Security,* Ch. 1, especially 21-22.

13   In Clarke A. Chambers, *Paul U. Kellogg and the Survey: Voices for Social Welfare and Social Justice* (Minneapolis, 1971), the relationship between welfare capitalism and social reform, strong especially in the 1920s, is noted. Kellogg, editor of the *Survey,* was intrigued by what he perceived as the advanced social views expressed especially by Edward Filene, Samuel Fels, and Gerard Swope.

14   The sections that follow will have reference to Perkins, *The Roosevelt I Knew,* especially 105-108, 278-300; Witte, *The Development of the Social Security Act;* Altmeyer, *The Formative Years of Social Security;* McKinley and Frase, *Launching Social Security;* George W. Martin, *Madam Secretary: Frances Perkins, A Biography of America's First Woman Cabinet Member* (Boston, 1976), 341-56; Searle F. Charles, *Minister of Relief: Harry Hopkins and the Great Depression* (Syracuse, 1963); Theron F. Schlabach, *E. E. Witte: Cautious Reformer* (Madison, 1969), especially Chs. 5-7; W. Andrew Achenbaum, *Old Age in the New Land: The American Experience Since 1790* (Baltimore, 1978), especially Ch. 7; David Hackett Fisher, *Growing Old in America* (New York, 1978), 182-85; Abraham Holtzman, *The Townsend Movement: A Political Study* (New York, 1963); Jackson K. Putnam, *Old-Age Politics in California: From Richardson to Reagan* (Stanford, 1970); Otis L. Graham, Jr., *An Encore for Reform: The Old Progressives and the New Deal* (New York, 1967); William Leuchtenburg, *Franklin D. Roosevelt and the New Deal* (New York, 1963);

Arthur M. Schlesinger, Jr., *The Coming of the New Deal* (Boston, 1959), Ch. 18, and *The Politics of Upheaval* (Boston, 1960), Ch. 3, and 613-14, 635-40. The fate of health insurance is a subject beyond the scope of this essay, but interested scholars should consult Daniel S. Hirshfield, *The Lost Reform: The Campaign for Compulsory Health Insurance in the United States from 1932 to 1942* (Cambridge, Mass., 1970). Chapter 7 of Douglas's *In the Fullness of Time: The Memoirs of Paul H. Douglas* (New York, 1972), reviews briefly his recollections of "The Struggle for Social Security and Labor Legislation." A thoughtful comparative overview is contained in Leonard Krieger, "The Idea of the Welfare State in Europe and the United States," *Journal of the History of Ideas*, 24 (Oct.-Dec. 1963), 553-68. Louis Leotta, "Abraham Epstein and the Movement for Old Age Security," *Labor History*, 16 (summer 1975), 359-77, concludes that although the depression was a "major impetus" to action, "a favorable climate of opinion toward social security legislation had already been created in the preceding decade and a half." A "small band of reformers operating through voluntary organizations" focused public awareness on the need for a national system of social insurance. For the influence of the radical rank-and-file wing of social work upon social insurance and other public policies, see Jacob Fisher's extended account, which mingles history and memoir: *The Response of Social Work to the Depression* (Boston, 1980). Criticism of the New Deal from the left, as reviewed by Fisher, anticipated the historical interpretation later proposed by Barton J. Bernstein, "The New Deal: The Conservative Achievements of Liberal Reform," in Bernstein, ed., *Towards a New Past* (New York, 1969), 263-88. On workmen's compensation, see Robert Asher, "Radicalism and Reform: State Insurance of Workmen's Compensation in Minnesota, 1910-1933," *Labor History*, 14 (winter 1973), 19-41, and his "Workmen's Compensation in the United States, 1880-1935," Ph.D. dissertation, University of Minnesota, 1971. A useful essay on mothers' assistance is Mark H. Leff, "Consensus for Reform: The Mothers' Pension Movement in the Progressive Era," *Social Science Review*, 47 (Sept. 1973), 397-417.

15 Frances Perkins, foreword in Witte, *The Development of the Social Security Act*, vi.

16 Holtzman, *The Townsend Movement*, 27, 87.

17 Remarks to the Conference on Economic Security, November 14, 1934, quoted in Witte, *Development of the Social Security Act*, 119. It is a nice irony that some congressional Republicans in 1981 have apparently adopted a strategy for revising social security that includes a shift away from the contributory principle and toward a shift of the financial burden to general tax revenues, a position vigorously proposed by left-of-center reformers and radicals in 1935—one imagines for quite different reasons!

18 Frank Bruno, *Trends in Social Work* (New York, 1957), 309.

19 Harry Hopkins, "Social Planning for the Future," *Social Service Review*, 8 (Sept. 1934), 407.

20 I have reference especially to the papers of the American Association of Social Workers (folders 195-232); the National Social Work Council (folders 67-68, 79, 82-85, 88 and Supplement folders 31-32, 41, 45-46, 63, 79, 112-113); Survey Associates (folders 352-353, 382, 424, 763-764, 799-800, 867-868); and to the personal papers of Paul U. Kellogg (folders 32-33, 141-143, 307, 338, 341-344), Helen Hall (folders 68-84, 107-108, 134, 244, 367, 375, 383, 386-387, legal folders 2-3), and Karl de Schweinitz (folders 96-97). The ephemeral records of diverse voluntary associations in human service fields—pamphlets, occasional publications, field studies, annual reports, newsletters, etc.—compose an additional and enormous body of evidence on the

policy roles of such agencies and societies over the past seventy years or so. These records are all on deposit at the Social Welfare History Archives Center.

21   These contributions during the depression and New Deal years are summarized in Chambers, *Paul U. Kellogg and the Survey*, Chs. 8-10. Kellogg and Helen Hall dissented from several features of the Report on Economic Security, 1935, and testified in favor of higher standards and a system that would give the federal government more authority over the states in the setting of benefits and other administrative matters; both of them, long-time supporters of social insurance, endorsed the bill in principle and then joined with other social work leaders in working for an amendment of the basic law.

22   Harry Lurie, "The Part Which Social Workers Have Taken in Promoting Social Legislation in New York State," *Proceedings of the National Conference of Social Work* (1935), 497-504.

23   Schlabach, *E. E. Witte*, 97.

From Pensions to Social Security: Social Insurance and the Rise of Dependency

William Graebner

WE ARE HERE today to determine why we have systems of social insurance, a term that includes old age insurance (what we commonly refer to as social security), unemployment insurance, and health insurance. The magnitude of the task before us is apparent even in the words that grace the program for this conference. We are to explore the "quest for security" by examining the origins of "social insurance." Here are ready-made answers: "security" on the one hand, "insurance" on the other. We must tolerate these and other terms that explain as well as label, including "social security" and the "welfare state." We use them because they are our heritage. But we should realize that this terminology is not neutral. Indeed, it is part of a structure of authority which legitimizes one view of these matters at the expense of others.[1]

In focusing my remarks today on old age insurance, I do so not simply because this is my field of scholarship but because, at the public level, at least, income maintenance expenditures related to old age dwarf those in other areas. "The welfare state," as Canadian scholar John Myles has put it, "is by and large a welfare state *for the elderly.*"[2]

I would like to begin by establishing a very general, and in some ways obvious, time frame for the rise of old age insurance. We can chart this development by the proliferation of private and public pension plans, the mechanism through which this program of "insurance" has been historically implemented. In the United States, service-related military pensions were first granted in 1861. Private corporate pension plans date to 1875, but as of 1932, only 15 percent of American workers were even potentially covered. Police pensions were common in larger cities by 1900, teachers' pensions by 1920. That same year, 1920, the federal government

---

William Graebner is Professor of History, State University of New York, College at Fredonia. Much of the material in this paper has been drawn from the author's *A History of Retirement,* copyright © Yale University Press, 1980.

offered pensions to some government workers with the Civil Service Retirement Act. Railroad workers secured a federal pension in 1935, the same year Franklin Roosevelt signed the Social Security Act. All forms of old age insurance—private, municipal, state, and federal—grew dramatically in the two decades after 1940.[3]

Roughly the same chronology emerges if we use another measure: the rate of participation of old people (over sixty-five) in the labor force—the Labor Force Participation Rate, or LFPR. This is an area of substantial disagreement. However, as I interpret the findings of other scholars, labor force participation rates for those over sixty-five declined between 1890 and 1930, but not very much. In 1930, nearly as large a percentage of males sixty-five years old and older were gainfully employed as in 1890. Between 1930 and 1940, the years of the Great Depression, the percentage fell dramatically. And it fell again, substantially, between 1940 and 1950.[4] In short, the over-sixty-five LFPR appears to move with the growth of old-age insurance. Each changes slowly before 1920 and rapidly between 1930 and 1950.

The correlation is there. The nature of the relationship between these two factors remains at issue. Let me suggest two scenarios, each of which might explain the data. In the first scenario, dependency is the problem, and social insurance is the solution. The mechanics are simple. Urban, industrial society is inhospitable to old people; it creates dependency—gradually at first, then, in the Great Depression, with a vengeance. In its early stages, this dependency problem could be treated through voluntary organizations and a few private, municipal, and state old age assistance programs. When these agencies proved inadequate in the depression, the federal government stepped in. According to this reading of history, the Social Security Act of 1935, like its antecedents, was created to solve a dependency crisis.[5]

The second scenario, which I shall defend here today, reverses the equation. According to this reading of history, social insurance creates dependency. That is, social insurance was designed to allow—in fact, to encourage—a substantial number of "capable" persons over age sixty, sixty-two, or sixty-five to exist without working, that is, to "retire." Before 1920, those who forged the pension systems that made up this network of social insurance had many goals in mind, none of them of transcendent importance. Therefore, they experimented widely with this new tool, retirement. After 1930, during the Great Depression, there obviously were many old persons who needed economic help. They got it through the old age assistance provisions of the Social Security Act. But the nation got something else. It got a long-term solution to unemployment, designed to institutionalize the modern old person, familiar to us all: workless, dependent on money payments—in a word, retired.[6] In the 1940s, business and labor created a massive private system of pension plans that had much the same function.

Social insurance for the aged, then, became of major importance in a statistical sense only in the 1940s, when it began to have a demonstrable impact on labor force participation among older persons. But the legislation that produced this impact, the Social Security Act, was not a child simply of depression thinking and conditions. Behind the legislation was a half century of experimentation with the mechanism of retirement—operating, as usual, through social insurance.

To describe this period of experimentation, I have selected three examples. Each illustrates an important function of retirement, and each helps reveal the links between dependency and social insurance.

The first example involves a retirement plan for teachers in nondenominational colleges, created in 1905 with a grant from Andrew Carnegie. Carnegie probably was most interested in helping undersalaried professors. But his choice to administer the arrangement, MIT's President Henry S. Pritchett, had other ideas. At MIT, Pritchett had advocated a pension system to keep younger men in service and, therefore, to stimulate "the development of the research spirit," which he considered vital to "national progress."[7] While Carnegie wanted a name for the organization that would reflect its narrow pension focus, Pritchett wanted one indicative of the agency's potential as a unifying mechanism for higher education. Pritchett prevailed. They settled on Carnegie Foundation for the Advancement of Teaching.[8]

Pritchett and Carnegie found common ground in their desire to invigorate higher education with a spirit of enterprise and efficiency. Superannuated professors could now be let go. And universities could use a pension plan to recruit persons to teaching who otherwise might have been tempted to seek careers in business or government.[9] But Pritchett went beyond Carnegie in his desire to create an organization that would encourage a socially responsible outlook in the professoriate.[10] Carnegie would have been satisfied with mere efficiency; Pritchett sought a kind of control.

Carnegie's papers contain many grateful letters from the near-impoverished professors who staffed the nation's colleges at the turn of the century.[11] We need deny neither this state of dependency, nor Carnegie's and Pritchett's interest in alleviating it, in order to suggest a more complex relationship between dependency and social insurance than these letters would imply. Pritchett did not leave the presidency of MIT to hold the hands of superannuated or needy professors. He joined Carnegie because he believed in the potential of social insurance as an instrument of efficiency and control in higher education. What he understood, in effect, was that the elimination of one kind of dependency created another (that is, retirement), and that this new dependency could be a source of social leverage. Grateful teachers, and grateful universities, could be shaped in a new image.

The second example of the uses of social insurance takes us into the federal bureaucracy, where turn-of-the-century efficiency experts battled a new enemy, old age. Retirement as we know it today did not exist. Therefore government agencies, like most public and private bureaucracies, served almost as old age homes. The U.S. Treasury in Washington, D.C., had 126 employees over age seventy, and 12 over eighty years of age.[12] (To some extent this was a "cohort" problem; that is, a problem produced by the aging of a group of Civil War veterans. As late as 1919, the Commissioner of Pensions claimed that 90 of his 878 employees had served in the Civil War.)[13] Supervisors, aware of the individual needs of those who worked under them, and in the absence of a pension system, often refused to fire aging employees, even when they were known to be unproductive.[14]

After 1895, this protective "community" came under attack. Its source was the secretary of the treasury. Under pressure because of mounting evidence of inefficiency in his department, he reduced the salaries of employees over age seventy and finally had to fire a large group of people defined as superannuated. In the Progressive Era, Presidents Roosevelt, Taft, and Wilson established commissions to grapple with the problems of efficiency in the government service, including those related to old age. One result was the Civil Service Retirement Act. Passed in 1920, it provided retirement pensions for employees aged seventy with fifteen or more years' experience. The act was a reaction against the continued influence of personal relationships in the federal bureaucracy. Its sponsors believed that supervisors would henceforth be more willing to remove aging or superannuated employees.[15]

In a sense, then, the law was a humane one, for it offered an alternative to being fired without a pension. But it is a strange kind of humanity which seeks to transform personal, human situations into bureaucratic ones. And that is what this social insurance legislation of 1920 was intended to do.

The law was not designed to alleviate dependency, except insofar as dependency was a product of bureau chiefs' firing older employees. Government workers had jobs; they had no compelling need for another kind of social insurance, the pension. Like the Carnegie pension system, the Civil Service Retirement Act *produced* a dependent population of persons who were retired or moving toward retirement.

This account of the social insurance movement in the civil service implies that "reform" was generated from above, by efficiency "experts," rather than from below, by government clerks and watchmen. However, there is evidence of a "democratic" component to civil service pensions. Three major organizations—the United States Civil Service Retirement Association (USCSRA), the National Association of Letter Carriers, and the National Association of Civil Service Employees—represented the interests of government workers during the two decades of political maneuvering that preceded the 1920 law.[16]

But if this is democracy, it is democracy operating within limits established outside its sphere of influence. That is, these employee organizations were created, and became essential, only after it had become apparent that some form of retirement was destined to replace the work environment as the primary support system for older government workers. The USCSRA was founded in 1900, but only *after* events at Treasury had made employees aware of their vulnerability. These organizations, and their quest for social insurance, illustrate not so much the demand for a new life-style called "retirement" as a defensive reaction against proponents of efficiency.

The third example, social insurance in railroading, may be viewed as a transition between the experimentation of the Progressive period and the Social Security Act. Although this example culminates in legislation signed two weeks after the Social Security Act of 1935, the first version of the law was passed before social security, in 1934. More to the point, the railroads had pioneered decades earlier in the development of social insurance for superannuated employees. Because these early plans were noncontributory, the roads sometimes used them to control workers or to break strikes. The aging work force of the 1920s made social insurance systems attractive as a way of facilitating the removal of inefficient older workers.[17]

In the Great Depression, another problem, employment, took precedence. Secretary of Labor Frances Perkins recommended, and Roosevelt signed, the Railroad Retirement Act of 1934, in part because of its anticipated impact on railroad unemployment and in part because it promised to increase efficiency by eliminating superannuated workers. Senator Robert Wagner agreed. He anticipated that the act would reduce unemployment by immediately retiring some fifty thousand railroad workers. Although Perkins, especially, understood that unemployment for railroad workers in 1934 often meant poverty, she did not justify the act to Roosevelt as a relief measure.[18] The 1934 *Report* of the Advisory Committee on Railroad Employment—whose signatories included J. Douglas Brown (later involved in creating social security), Alvin Hansen, Isador Lubin, Sumner Slichter, Walton Hamilton, and other "liberal" luminaries—claimed that a retirement annuity system was essential because present systems had neither effected "necessary retirements" nor given proper support to railroad workers. A new retirement system was required, the report said, to encourage retirement of older workers and to increase opportunity for younger men.[19] Moreover, the ensuing court battle over the constitutionality of the law was fought over the issue of whether the creation of "employment opportunity" was constitutionally viable. The Supreme Court would accept the legislation only after it was recast within a framework of security, based on the general welfare clause of the Constitution. In other words, the act was not originally passed because of a desire to "insure" railroad workers against future hazards (a description of social "insurance").[20] Rather, the law was designed to affect employment and efficiency, and to do so immediately. Short- and long-term, the goal was a less crowded labor market.

Finally, we come to the Social Security Act of 1935. Here, indeed, is one of the untouchables of American history, a law so shrouded in the liberal mythology of the welfare state that we no longer ask why the act was passed. We know why. Old age insurance became law, so the story goes, because an enormous population of dependent or potentially dependent older persons needed long-term security from unpredictable economic hazards.[21]

Without throwing out the baby with the bathwater, I would suggest another interpretation of social security, particularly of its old age insurance provisions: the Social Security Act was a piece of *retirement* legislation. It was consciously designed to accomplish what other retirement legislation had accomplished—the removal of older persons from the work force.

The evidence for this position takes three forms. First, "direct" evidence, which consists largely of an account of the process of creating the social security system; second, "indirect" evidence, including summaries of the history of retirement and of the New Deal's response to the Townsend movement; and third, "logical" evidence (though some will question the logic).

The old age insurance portion of the Social Security Act was created and drafted in the Committee on Economic Security (CES), appointed by Roosevelt in 1934. Within the CES, four persons played a prominent role: Barbara Armstrong, a professor of law; Murray Latimer, a member of the Railroad Retirement Board, author of a study of industrial pension systems, and head of a firm called Industrial Relations Counselors, Inc.; J. Douglas Brown, an economist with the Industrial Relations Section at Princeton University, who had worked with Latimer on a national railroad pension plan; and Otto Richter, an actuary from AT&T. Neither Edwin Witte, the titular head of the Committee on Economic Security, nor Arthur Altmeyer, assistant secretary of labor and chairman of the Technical Board of the CES, had much to do with the drafting—and, I am tempted to say, conceptualization—of the legislation.[22] Wilbur Cohen, Witte's research assistant in 1934, argues that the tenor of the CES was shaped by an industrial relations, as opposed to a welfare, outlook: "The roots of the social insurance movement," recalled Cohen, "came out of the work and consideration of the people in the field of labor legislation. Social insurance was to them a form of remedial legislation to deal with the problems of labor unrest and industrial society which grew out of labor-management problem[s]."[23] Armstrong and Brown concur on the extraordinary independence of the aggressive core of the CES.[24]

Armstrong's oral history memoir, compiled in 1965, leaves little doubt that national old age insurance was conceived with retirement in mind. Roosevelt, she argues, had to choose between keeping older workers in jobs, on the one hand, and creating opportunities and hope for youth, on the other: "The interest of Mr. Roosevelt was with the younger man. And to that extent, I went along. . . . We knew as we sat and planned this work that there were two reasons why Mr. Roosevelt had acted at all. One was great concern for the unemployment problem, and the young people were without hope and without a chance for earnings. And we, if possible, were expected to work out a program that would help both, and that's what we did."[25]

One method of securing the desired labor market impact was the "retirement test." When the House passed a bill lacking such a provision, Roosevelt publicly announced his position: retirement should be a condition of the granting of any annuity. The Senate committee working on its version of the legislation assumed that a retirement test would be added.[26] Accounts by Armstrong and Cohen confirm that the retirement test as finally constituted ($15 per month was the maximum one could earn without losing social security benefits) was an outgrowth of depression conditions. "That's why that ridiculous amount of $15 was put in," Armstrong recalled. "Let him earn some pin money, but it had to be on *retirement*. And retirement means that you've stopped working for pay." Although those who drafted the act were concerned with providing economic security to retired persons, there was never any doubt that those persons had to be retired to receive benefits. "He would not get *retirement* benefits unless he retired," said Armstrong. "We *never* called these benefits anything but retirement benefits."[27]

Brown and Armstrong disagree on whether organized labor pressed for social insurance that would have a labor market impact. "There had been heavy unemployment," Brown recalled, "and to the extent that you could explain this to labor, they would certainly be for a plan that would take men out of the labor market when they were superannuated." According to Armstrong, however, organized labor "never said a word about it." But, she added, "this labor market idea was in the minds of Latimer, Brown, Armstrong and Richter, and it was in the mind, I think, of anybody who ever worked on social insurance."[28]

Although much of the business community was reluctant to support a national old age insurance program, progressive elements of business, represented in the Advisory Council to the CES, did support it. The crucial figure was Marion Folsom of Eastman Kodak. Kodak's experience with older workers and pensions had made Folsom believe that federal old age insurance could help corporations shed the superannuated by providing employees with adequate retirement income. As a member of the Advisory Council, Folsom stressed the contribution old age insurance could make to corporate efficiency. By encouraging employees to plan for retirement and to retire, social "security" would increase productivity.[29]

CES testimony before Congress confirms and enlarges upon the oral history sources. Because Armstrong was known for her acerbic personality, much of the task of giving this testimony fell to Brown and Latimer. Before the Senate Finance Committee, Brown claimed that the CES had insisted on worker contributions to the system not only to establish the contractual right of a worker to his annuity, but also to insure that the annuity would be large enough to induce the retirement of superannuated workers. For maximum labor market impact, Brown and others working with the CES favored compulsory retirement at age sixty-five. Of particular concern was the need to find some mechanism to increase the employment opportunity of those over forty-five years of age.[30]

Murray Latimer was one of a few persons with a well-developed historical perspective to appear before the Congress. He understood that the Railroad Retirement Act and the Civil Service Retirement Act were precedents for the pending old age insurance system, and he attempted to explain to the Senate committee the mechanisms by which these laws induced or compelled retirement. Latimer's prepared statement surveyed the disruptive impact of older workers, employed and seeking employment, on wage rates, efficiency, and work prospects of younger people in the labor market. He was distressed at the legislation then being considered because the level of pensions provided, "even if raised considerably above existing standards, would not be high enough to induce any considerable voluntary withdrawals from the labor market; nor would employers be able to retire superannuated employees without friction." Larger benefits were vital under a contributory system, Latimer argued, because collections would necessarily begin when employees were young and dependency a remote possibility. These younger employees would expect their contributions to purchase not only future annuities but the removal of older workers and an increase in the rate of promotion.[31] Latimer's final statement on the relationship between benefits and employment impact under the impending legislation reveals ambivalence:

Whether the relation between the two initially is reasonable I do not know, it is a matter of judgment; but nevertheless in my own judgment the annuities set in this act are to be regarded as minima amounts rather than maxima for the purpose which the system is supposed to accomplish, namely, the protection of the aged group, their removal from employment, and the quick supplanting of what we think is a system which would be unsatisfactory in the long run.[32]

In short, Latimer believed that, as constructed, the system would not have much employment impact. He did, however, see the old age provisions of the Social Security Act as part of the history of retirement, with all its labor market implications. And he expected the system to take its place within that retirement history at some point in the future, when benefits were increased.

Other provisions of old age insurance were also designed within a labor-market context. For reasons of cost, the CES rejected suggestions that the retirement age be lowered below sixty-five; it resisted a higher age of sixty-eight or seventy—the latter was then common in state old age pension programs—because of anticipated congressional and public opposition to late retirement in a period of high unemployment. The act also operated to discourage over-sixty-five employment by subjecting earnings for such workers to taxation for social security purposes (under Title VIII) but not counting earnings after that age in determining benefits.[33]

Within limits, the Congress was receptive to these arguments. In the House, a motion to recommit the Doughton bill (H.R. 7260) in order to reduce the age of eligibility from sixty-five to sixty (among other purposes) received over 160 votes. The measure's sponsor in the Senate, Robert Wagner, opened debate in June, 1935, by offering a number of suggestions he thought would appeal to business. "The incentive to the retirement of superannuated workers," he argued, "will improve efficiency standards, will make new places for the strong and eager, and will increase the productivity of the young by removing from their shoulders the uneven burden of caring for the old." In his public addresses Wagner made clear his belief that even in normal times technology would create a group of four to six million able-bodied unemployed. Retirement compensation could be used to secure "the withdrawal of those who are older and less efficient, and who deserve and want a few years of rest."[34]

There are several problems with this "direct" evidence. One is that it is not all that plentiful, especially considering the mass of information and testimony generated by the issue of old age insurance in the 1930s. Another lies in the conflicting nature of some of the evidence. Brown, for example, testified about labor market impact and mentioned it in his oral history, but his recent book ignores it.[35] Armstrong's oral history account seems incontrovertible, yet her 1932 book, *Insuring the Essentials*, is silent on the issue.[36] Moreover, there is some question as to how much weight should be assigned to the views of a handful of persons associated with the Committee on Economic Security.

There is no easy way to resolve these evidential problems. What we can do is attempt to determine whether these ideas about retirement and labor market impact made sense in some larger historical framework, and whether they were part of a general cultural understanding. And that requires what I term "indirect" evidence. The most important form of such evidence is that developed earlier in this essay: the evidence that well before 1935 the history of social insurance was inseparable from the history of retirement, labor markets, and efficiency. It seems unlikely that a national program of social insurance could have been put in place that did not take account of, or build upon, this history.

A second type of indirect evidence emerges from the relationship between the Townsend pension movement and the New Deal. Historians generally agree that the Roosevelt administration developed its social security program in the shadow of this grass-roots movement.[37] To the extent that this was true, Roosevelt and his aides must have been conscious of the importance of the labor market issue and of the relationship between retirement and the labor market. The popularity of the Townsend program was closely related to the labor market claims of its proponents.[38] Therefore, undercutting the Townsend movement meant, among other things, demonstrating that the administration's program of social security would have labor market impact. Latimer made this clear in his testimony before the Senate Finance Committee. "It is not necessary," he said, "to go to the fantastic lengths of the Townsend plan to get the stimulus for that removal [of older workers from the labor market]."[39]

Finally, it is possible to achieve a kind of understanding of the origins of old age insurance apart from what people said about it and apart from the frameworks in which they conceptualized the problem. This requires that we retrieve an issue posed earlier in this essay: the relationship between social insurance and labor force participation rates. The decline in over sixty-five LFPR between 1930 and 1940 might well be explained by pervasive unemployment, as more and more older persons were discouraged from seeking work. But this would not explain why rates remained low and dropped further in succeeding decades.

Two factors account for this long-term decline in LFPR. One factor was what I have elsewhere called the "selling of retirement"— a broadbased effort to market retirement as a new life-style.[40] The other was the combination of incentives to retirement provided by old age assistance, old age insurance, and private pensions.[41] If we conclude that social security had this labor market impact, is it possible, or likely, that it was not *intended* to have it? Does it make sense to argue that the life-style of retirement was a historical accident, the outgrowth of a policy designed simply to bestow security?

I think not. At the very least, social security was *allowed* to produce retirement. Until the 1970s, no significant effort was made to encourage older workers to return to, or remain in, the labor market.[42] Whatever else it was, national old age insurance was also an instrument of retirement. The Congress, the president, the business community, and the people who drafted the legislation at the Committee on Economic Security knew this. They knew it because nothing made more sense amidst the severe unemployment of the Great Depression, and because they understood, in different degrees, perhaps, the historic relationship between old age insurance and retirement. They knew it because they understood, and even appreciated, that social insurance produced a new and useful form of dependency.

NOTES

1   Important recent statements on the problem of covert authority include Richard Sennett, *Authority* (New York, 1980); Michel Foucault, *Power/Knowledge: Selected Interviews and Other Writings, 1972-1977*, ed. by Colin Gordon (New York, 1980); and William Warner, "A First draft toward stating the Potentials of the Artist's Book as reflected in its recent near history and its new Future" (unpublished paper).

2   John F. Myles, "The Aged and the Welfare State: An Essay in Political Demography" (paper presented at the meeting of the International Sociological Association, Research Committee on Aging, Paris, July 8-9, 1981), 3. Myles's emphasis.

3   William Graebner, *A History of Retirement: The Meaning and Function of an American Institution, 1885-1978* (New Haven, 1980), especially 132-34.

4   Brian J. Gratton, "Urban Elders, 1890-1950: Work, Family, and Dependency in Boston" (Ph.D. dissertation, Boston University, 1980), Ch. 3. Cf. W. Andrew Achenbaum, *Old Age in the New Land: The American Experience since 1790* (Baltimore, 1978), 102-03. LFPR is a measure of potential participation, not actual employment. Prior to the 1940 census, however, the work force was defined as all "gainfully occupied" workers — workers who usually followed a "gainful occupation," though perhaps unemployed at the time of the census. The 1940 census definition of the labor force included the employed and the unemployed who were *actively* seeking work.

5   This is the standard account. See, for example, David Hackett Fischer, *Growing Old in America* (New York, 1977), Ch. 4; Harold Wilensky, *The Welfare State and Equality* (Berkeley, 1975); Achenbaum, *Old Age in the New Land*, Ch. 7; and the discussion of pluralist views in Myles, "Aged and the Welfare State," pp. 2, 7-8.

6 Myles, "Aged and the Welfare State," argues a similar case using somewhat different tools.

7 Clipping, "Teachers' Pensions," *Boston Globe*, Feb. 20, 1904, Henry S. Pritchett Papers, Box 18, "Scrapbooks—1904 Miscell.," Library of Congress, Washington, D.C. For a fuller account of the Carnegie pension system, see Graebner, *Retirement*, 108-19 and Joseph Frazier Wall, *Andrew Carnegie* (New York, 1970), 870-80.

8 Pritchett to Carnegie, Dec. 9, 1905, Carnegie to Pritchett, Dec. 11, 1905, Carnegie Papers, Box 122, Library of Congress.

9 L. Clark Seelye to Carnegie, April 20, 1905, Box 115; Samuel Lantz to Carnegie, April 29, 1905, Box 116; W. Peterson to Carnegie, April 19, 1905, Box 115; E. Benjamin Andrews to Carnegie, April 19, 1905, Box 118. All in Carnegie Papers; Pritchett to Carnegie, Jan. 21, 1908, Box 2, file "Andrew Carnegie, 1901-1913," Pritchett Papers.

10 Carnegie Foundation for the Advancement of Teaching, *Eleventh Annual Report of the President and of the Treasurer*, Oct. 1916 (Boston, n.d.), 62.

11 See, for example, Edwin B. Davis to Carnegie, April 28, 1905, Box 115, Carnegie Papers.

12 U.S. Department of Commerce and Labor, Bureau of the Census, *The Executive Civil Service of the United States*, Bulletin No. 12 (Washington, D.C., 1904), 28 (table 24), 35 (tables 31,32).

13 U.S. Congress, Senate, Committee on Civil Service and Retrenchment, *Retirement of Civil Service Employees: Hearings Before the Committee on Civil Service and Retrenchment on S. 1699, A bill for the Retirement of Employees in the Classified Civil Service and for other purposes*, 66th Cong., 1st sess. (Washington, D.C., 1919), pp. 10-11. On the problem of cohort in the history of old age, see Gratton, "Urban Elders," pp. 123-29.

14 "Answers to the Keep Commission," a bound volume, in Record Group 28, "Records of the Post Office Department," Office of the Postmaster General (PGO), series 19 (Records Relating to the Keep Commission, 1906-1907), National Archives, Washington, D.C.

15 Graebner, *Retirement*, 60, 80-81.

16 *Ibid.*, 61-63, 67-71.

17 *Ibid.*, 132, 154. See, for example, U. S. Congress, House, Committee on Labor, *Old Age Pensions: Hearings Before the Committee on Labor*, 71st Cong., 2d sess., Feb. 20, 21, 28, 1930 (Washington, D.C., 1930), pp. 140-41, 152; and Dan H. Mater, "Effects of Seniority Upon the Welfare of the Employee, the Employer and Society," *Journal of Business*, 14 (Oct. 1941), 338.

18 Graebner, *Retirement*, Ch. 6. Important sources include Perkins to Roosevelt, June 22, 1934, Record Group 174, "Records of the Department of Labor," Office of the Secretary, General Subject Files, 1933-40, Box 11, file "Bills Before Congress, 1934, Miscellaneous," National Archives; *New York Times*, July 1, 1934, p. 1; Wagner to Roosevelt, June 23, 1934, Robert F. Wagner Papers, Box 327, file 19, Georgetown University Library, Washington, D.C.

19 Advisory Committee on Railroad Employment, *Report*, in Otto Beyer Papers, Box 47, file "Advisory Committee on Railroad Employment. Report of the Committee," Library of Congress.

20   Graebner, *Retirement*, 159-63. See especially *New York Times*, Aug. 14, 1934, pp. 1, 6, May 16, 1935, p. 33, May 18, 1935, p. 23.

21   On the historiography of social security, see Graebner, *Retirement*, 181-83. Among the studies which accept this view are Arthur M. Schlesinger, Jr., *The Coming of the New Deal* (Boston, 1958); William Leuchtenburg, *Franklin D. Roosevelt and the New Deal* (New York, 1963); and Achenbaum, *Old Age in the New Land.*

22   J. Douglas Brown, "The American Philosophy of Social Insurance," in *Social Security: Programs, Problems, and Policies*, ed. by William Haber and Wilbur J. Cohen (Homewood, Ill., 1960), 8, 15; Barbara Armstrong Memoir, 1965, Columbia University Oral History Collection, Columbia University, Vol. I, pp. 104, 46-47.

23   Wilbur Cohen Memoir, 1966, Columbia University Oral History Collection, pp. 34-35. Altmeyer adds the interesting suggestion that social security was shaped by people who had worked on war risk insurance during World War I. Arthur Altmeyer Oral History Memoir, 1967, Columbia University Oral History Collection, Vol. II, p. 153.

24   Brown, "American Philosophy," 17; Armstrong Memoir, I, 46-47, 104.

25   Armstrong Memoir, II, 255, 261.

26   Edwin E. Witte, *The Development of the Social Security Act: A Memorandum on the History of the Committee on Economic Security and Drafting and Legislative History of the Social Security Act* (Madison, 1962; composed in the mid-1930s), 160.

27   Armstrong Memoir, II, 257. Armstrong's emphasis. See also Wilbur Cohen in *Problems of Aging: Transactions of the Fourteenth Conference*, 7-8 (Sept. 1951), St. Louis, Mo., ed. by Nathan Shock (Caldwell, N.J., 1952), pp. 86-87.

28   J. Douglas Brown Memoir, 1970, Columbia University Oral History Collection, p. 115; Armstrong Memoir, II, 260.

29   Armstrong Memoir, II, 80-81; Marion B. Folsom Memoir, 1965, Columbia University Oral History Collection, Vol. 1, pp. 78, 130, 46-47, 63. See also Edward Berkowitz and Kim McQuaid, "Businessman and Bureaucrat: The Evolution of the American Social Welfare System, 1900-1940," *Journal of Economic History* 30 (March 1978), 130-40.

30   U.S. Congress, Senate, Committee on Finance, *Economic Security Act: Hearings on S. 1130*, A Bill to Alleviate the Hazards of Old Age Unemployment, Illness, and Dependency, to Establish a Social Insurance Board in the Department of Labor, to Raise Revenue, and for Other Purposes, 74th Cong., 1st sess. (Washington, D.C., 1935), pp. 282-83.

31   *Ibid*, pp. 755, 744-45.

32   *Ibid.*, pp. 746-49.

33   Wilbur J. Cohen, *Retirement Policies Under Social Security: A Legislative History of Retirement Ages, the Retirement Test and Disability Benefits* (Berkeley, 1957), 3, 18, 19; *Congressional Record*, 74th Cong., 1st sess., 1935, v. 79, pt. 9, p. 9536; Armstrong Memoir, II, 256.

34   U. S. Congress, House, *Congressional Record*, 74th Cong., 1st sess., 1935, v. 79, pt. 9, p. 9286 (Wagner's Senate statement); J. Joseph Huthmacher, *Senator Robert F. Wagner and the Rise of Urban Liberalism* (New York, 1971), 177.

35 Brown's *Essays on Social Security* (Princeton, 1977) treats the 1937/38 Advisory Council on Social Security, which Brown chaired. His discussion, however, ignores the council's stated desire to encourage retirement by increasing benefits: "The policy of paying higher benefits to persons retiring in earlier years of the statute than are the equivalent of the individual contributions is already established in the present Act. Such a policy is not only sound social insurance practice but has long been recognized as necessary in private pension programs. *Only through the payment of reasonable benefits can older workers be retired.*" Advisory Council on Social Security, "Final Report" (Dec. 10, 1938), appended to Brown, *Essays*, 21-22. (My emphasis.)

36 Barbara Armstrong, *Insuring the Essentials: Minimum Wage and Social Insurance—A Living Wage Program* (New York, 1932).

37 Fischer, *Growing Old*, pp. 182-83; Leuchtenburg, *Roosevelt and the New Deal*, 131; Frances Perkins, *The Roosevelt I Knew* (New York, 1946), 294.

38 For example, see Mrs. Mary T. Elliott to Roosevelt, May 21, 1934, Box 2, Official File 494A, "Old Age Pensions, 1933-45," Franklin Delano Roosevelt Library, Hyde Park, New York.

39 Senate, Committee on Finance, *Economic Security Act: Hearings*, p. 746.

40 Graebner, *Retirement*, 231-34.

41 *Ibid.*, 215-26; Myles, "Aged and the Welfare State," 21-35.

42 When that effort did come, it occurred in the context of international challenges to American economic hegemony and fears of bankruptcy for the social security system. See Graebner, *Retirement*, Ch. 9.

Herbert Hoover's Planning for Unemployment and Old Age Insurance Coverage, 1921 to 1933

Vaughn Davis Bornet

THE HERBERT HOOVER presented in this essay is the humanitarian concerned with planning for the long-range welfare of the people of the United States. Little has been known about the desires, hopes, and plans of Secretary of Commerce and President Hoover in the area the public has come to call social welfare. This is true even though he and several close associates later asserted that those years did in fact witness thought and action by them on behalf of payments and pensions for the unemployed and the aged. The Hoover interest, when mentioned, has been given minimum space. Never, so far as I have learned, has there been any effort to place the Hoover ideas in the context of at least some of the national social welfare experience.

My interest in social welfare goes back a quarter of a century and my research on Hoover longer than that. Invited to explore this area of concern, I have tried to piece together a story that ultimately surprised me and that should be new and useful to scholars, students, and the interested and receptive part of the public. For Hoover did in fact leave a record of dreams and efforts in this humanitarian area, just as he did in so many others.

This article will take up, in order, his plans and work in the field of insurance for the unemployed; his attitude toward state-funded old age payments and social insurance framed on the overseas model; and his attempts to stimulate interest in private annuities for the aged. His commissioning of a study of American society will be seen here to have been designed to further practical welfare goals. But his reaction in later years to the Social Security Act of 1935 and its amendments has been omitted because of lack of space and its remoteness from the events portrayed here.

It is possible to take a broad view of Hoover and society by observing at some length that Hoover once worked to insure the social well-being of Americans caught in Europe at the outbreak of World

Vaughn Davis Bornet is Emeritus Professor of History and Social Science, Southern Oregon State College, and resides in Ashland, Oregon.

War I; that he placed American agriculture in a position to supply much of the food intake of European society; and that while the displaced and hungry after two world wars had no insurance arrangement with this nation, Hoover saw to it that we acted as though they did. He also performed the same role in 1940-41 as much as he could, despite official opposition, while the Nazis roamed over the continent. By no means finally, when working with the Boys Clubs, he certainly thought he was guaranteeing a better life for underprivileged boys. It was logical that he would become a member of the board of a giant life insurance company in the 1930s, and not for the honorarium, for he firmly believed in deterring personal and family catastrophe by planning ahead. Hoover cherished the conviction that some personal sacrifice might reasonably be expected of all who hope to insure themselves a comfortable life during their senior years in the social system.

Many questions come to mind. One of the most interesting, of course, is this: Would the United States have gotten some form of unemployment insurance and old age protection if Hoover had continued as president from 1933 to 1937? His plans for achieving such a goal were steadily maturing and depended on the pieces coming together at the right moment, so the answer appears to be: yes. But he really hoped to make substantial progress in his first term, as will be seen directly.

BEGINNING in 1921, Secretary of Commerce Hoover explored in some detail the possibility of providing World War I veterans with sickness and unemployment insurance, old age pensions, and support of dependents after the veteran's death. Much of his exploration took the form of questioning top executives of the life insurance industry, an industry in which Hoover placed great faith then and later.[1] Before moving to further stages of Hoover's activity, it may be well to consider that in dealing with the American life insurance industry in the 1920s, Hoover was interacting with an industry possibly second only to the United States government in assets. New York Life had long led the world in ordinary insurance, exclusive of industrial, but in 1922 it was just being passed by Metropolitan Life Insurance Company. The activities of the latter at that time are impressive even now: over 25 million policies in force ($7 billion in amount; company assets were $1 billion); 19.5 million lives covered, amounting to a sixth of the American and Canadian population; income was $350 million. (The national debt at the time was $22.8 billion and federal expenditures for the year just finished were but $5.5 billion.) Metropolitan was engaged in group insurance and welfare work (including some free nursing for industrial policy holders).[2]

Unemployment insurance was a concern of an industrial conference called by President Wilson in 1919, a meeting which included Hoover as vice-chairman. In their report of March 6, 1920, the conferees mildly suggested that "good industrial management on the part of a nation" would involve agencies providing against illness, old age, premature death, and industrial accident. The subject should be investigated, they concluded. Soon the new secretary of commerce would try to interest Wesley C. Mitchell, of the National Bureau of Economic Research, in studying various aspects of unemployment. This would be followed up a year later with still another request for research, which resulted in the study, *Business Cycles and Unemployment.* A study of unemployment insurance was also contemplated.[3]

Hoover went well beyond this in a long letter to Samuel Gompers, president of the American Federation of Labor, on October 23, 1920. This Hoover letter, deriving from personal conversation a few days before, said it was possible to increase production by 5 to 30 percent if workers had an attitude toward work which would maximize production and minimize strikes and lockouts. Unfortunately, increased production—though beneficial in the long run—could decrease employment "in the short view." Thus there would have to be a "collective bargain" between employers and employee organizations. He thought there needed to be "monetary guarantees" on both sides; from this could come "the provision of unemployment and sickness insurance" on an adequate scale. Employers would surely be ready "to inaugurate a joint insurance against unemployment and sickness," if by a collective bargain increased devotion to production would result. Like Gompers, Hoover believed in voluntary action rather than government interference.[4]

Now Hoover turned to Metropolitan Life Insurance Company with a public proposal that it institute unemployment insurance after appropriate study. Metropolitan was an inevitable choice, since the company had been trying in vain since 1919 to get the New York State Senate insurance committee to permit private life insurance companies to write such policies. In those years the superintendent of insurance thought it "socialism"—at least, "the entering wedge." He had also charged that there was limited data, but this was precisely what the company sought to gather.[5] Hoover met with Metropolitan's president, Harley Fiske, in August, 1922.

There was some interest in the subject of unemployment insurance at the time. Professor Leo Wolman had spoken to the subject, and books had been written about it. Said actuary James D. Craig in 1923: "It has been discussed at length in the press, reported upon by Chambers of Commerce, debated before the National Civic Federation and presented for legislation in certain states. Among the various influences there is probably none which should focus the attention of the Actuarial Society of America more than the interest taken in it by Mr. Herbert Hoover." Craig's article on the subject urged the private insurance industry to pay attention to what the secretary of commerce was suggesting. After all, payments to those out of work went back to ancient times. Still, "Compulsory Unemployment Insurance does not seem to be popular with the press, employers, employees or taxpayers."[6] So there was real disagreement on what to do; here was fertile soil for Hoover leadership.

The secretary of commerce made his big push on unemployment insurance in an address to the Metropolitan Life Insurance Company managers' conference on January 27, 1923. A premise was that keeping this kind of program in the private sector would be to avoid "the blighting hand of government." After all, "Unemployment insurance in the hands of the Government would bring the disaster of incompetent and vicious encroachment of bureaucracy into the daily lives of our people." Employers, however, could presumably band into large groups that would cooperate with the insurance companies. Here was one of the great fields "where insurance can be newly developed, where if scientifically employed, founded on a basis of actual savings, [and] contributed to by the employer, [the insurers] would provide one of those great safeguards against suffering and add to our social stability." Repeatedly Hoover spoke of "service" and of "mutuality." If his advice should be heeded, these would temper individualism "in such a way as to preserve its great qualities and at the same time safeguard it from destruction." The insurance men in his audience were impressed. They recognized, as others did at the time, that "the task is one of almost inconceivable magnitude," he would remember. "However, the companies did not wish even to experiment with it."[7] (This judgment of years later was too harsh, for the companies faced an insurmountable problem with the bureaucrats and politicians of New York State, as we shall see.)

Now Hoover wrote to Samuel Gompers along the line of his Metropolitan talk, pointing out that since mutual insurance companies had representatives everywhere, "it would not add greatly to their overhead" to write policies. These might be issued directly to the worker, and "in many cases employers would contribute to the premiums by way of payment directly to the Insurance Company upon presentation of evidence to them of some measure of payment by the employee." The result would be increased saving, sustained income in time of depression—and accompanying buying power resulting in less acute depressions. He tried to reassure the aged Gompers that, after all, here were "none of the objectives of governmental insurance." Each man could participate as much as he would. So there would be "no limitation of individual liberty, no obligation and no charity about it." Thus there would be a "reservist employee," one laid off, to be sure, in depression but destined to come back when business revived. Such a man deserved support for being part of such a reserve. Hoover was clearly wasting his time with Gompers, who had long been allergic to government programs, but he ended his letter hopefully: "The matter needs careful working out but I believe that with the good will and support of some of the great companies, there is the possibility of useful development." A year later, according to Fiske, Gompers apparently labored "under a misunderstanding as to the purposes and effects of the Unemployment Insurance Bill which has been introduced in the New York Legislature." Fiske even had a member of the legislature all set to accompany the Metropolitan actuary on a visit to Gompers, but the legislator backed out.[8]

The fiscal year 1923-24 saw Metropolitan studying the Hoover unemployment insurance idea and struggling to get a new facilitating bill through the legislature. It failed to get clearance from insurance department officials at first but then won them over when there was a new committee chairman to work with. When the Joint Insurance Committee met on the subject, the only objection heard was from the trade unions. Gompers even wrote a letter of opposition. The chairman of the Assembly Insurance Committee had his own reasons for opposing it; wouldn't Hoover write him, asked Fiske—who was terribly embarrassed when the secretary of commerce wrote that "by long established custom, Federal Cabinet Officers are inhibited from addressing themselves to state legislatures regarding matters within their province."[9] Under the circumstances obtaining in New York State (which housed the big insurance companies), with the companies insisting on what the chairman of the legislative committee thought to be a "vague" bill, no adjustment between the industry and the legislators could be reached.

The bill—the Phelps bill, introduced February 22, 1924—need not further concern us here, but the fact that a full page of enabling legislation was needed before private insurers could write unemployment policies in the nation's largest state in the mid-1920s is not generally recognized and must not go unnoticed.[10] But the denial itself was touch and go. Few important matters in history, perhaps, have been settled so casually and obscurely. The Senate passed the bill handily, forty to seven. On the last day of the session the superintendent of insurance very belatedly supported it. After an all night session and much confusion, it turned out that the bill had died in the Assembly Committee. Metropolitan would continue its work on a policy, however, although far too many diluting safeguards were put into it. Said Fiske to his fellow life insurance company presidents late in 1925, "Patience, patience—as sure as God spares my life, we are going to issue unemployment insurance." It would only be in 1928 that the approval of William Green and Matthew Woll of the American Federation of Labor would be given to the concept, but economic events clearly intervened.[11]

Meanwhile, companies or associations of employers had in a few cases conducted their own experiments at setting up unemployment plans in conjunction with their employees. This practice began in 1921 with the Cleveland Garment Manufacturers Association and the Ladies' Garment Workers' Union; surety bonds guaranteed performance. In April, 1923, the Chicago Industrial Federation and the Amalgamated Clothing Workers reached agreement, using an unemployment reserve fund managed by a board of trustees. The advantages of the Hoover approach over these can be weighed. By 1926 there were about four hundred formal pension plans in industry, according to Abraham Epstein; these covered over four million workers—but only 17.2 percent of the nonagricultural gainfully employed. The non-contributory plans paid about $400 a year and the others a third more. In 1931 in Rochester, New York, there was set up by fourteen companies, employing from forty-five workers to thirteen thousand, an unemployment benefit plan under which a substantial reserve would be built up voluntarily and independently, rather than by the use of government. The companies hoped that by 1933 the reserve would be sufficient to begin paying benefits. Another hope was that the allocation of 1 to 2 percent of payroll per year to such a fund would turn out to be enough.[12] Meanwhile, the General Electric Company was working on its own unemployment plan, based on contributions by the company and employees. The experimental plan was described to President Hoover by Gerard Swope, president of GE, as early as June 20, 1930.[13]

Unemployment insurance was making only slow progress by the time of the Hoover presidency, it appears. In 1931, Frederick Ecker, Fiske's successor as president of Metropolitan, wrote Hoover that the legal problem in his state continued to be a roadblock. If the law should ever be amended to permit it, the company would be willing "to experiment with groups in selected industries."[14] Experimenting meant coverage for only some workers. The politicians saw this as undemocratic or had other objections; the companies, entrusted with people's insurance payments, naturally wanted to select good risks, at least until sure of their ground. Ecker wrote Hoover how far Metropolitan had traveled toward meeting pension needs by writing group policies with employers. "You said you would be interested," he began, recalling that he had said Metropolitan was writing such policies all along. Standard Oil of New York had just covered forty-five thousand employees with retirement annuities, life insurance, accidental death and dismemberment insurance, and total and permanent disability benefits. "We are finding a growing desire on the part of employers to provide protection to employees against old age dependency," he asserted. But the possibility of unemployment insurance coverage was getting more attention.[15]

From this we see that early in the Hoover presidency the dream of unemployment insurance handled by giant life insurance companies was not dead in the minds of either Ecker or Hoover. As a matter of fact, the Metropolitan president (undoubtedly under the stimulus from the White House) was now prepared to send a vice-president and the company actuary abroad in summer, 1931, "to study the situation in England and on the continent of Europe. This is with a view of getting at first hand the views, opinions and conclusions of the governmental authorities, of employers, and of labor." The resulting study would have great value, Ecker thought, and would provide more authoritative data and information than was then available. The only reason he had told the president all this, he said, was because of "your expressed interest." Hoover, who knew that a book-writing project he had instituted with a professional writer to do just this had fallen through (see below), replied that he was indeed "deeply interested in the subject" and hoped to be kept informed.[16]

Research began within Metropolitan in fall, 1930, on the overall subject of social insurance as practiced abroad. Proof that Hoover was responsible for this activity is lacking, but the timing seems significant. The first short monograph appeared in January, 1931. On March 30, President Ecker was again invited to spend a night at the White House. There the subjects under discussion were the social insurance picture abroad, Hoover's continuing interest in insurance for the elderly and unemployed, and the coming overseas research investigation. Showing the importance he attached to the trip, the president furnished each of the travelers with three letters of introduction to the American ambassadors in London, Berlin, and Rome. "In view of the prominence which this issue [social insurance] has been given in the United States," he wrote, "I am anxious that these gentlemen shall have every facility obtainable in examining the social results of such activities in the country to which you are accredited as their reports will have great value to the Administration." The report of the three travelers, who were major figures at Metropolitan, would soon be published in the company's social insurance series.[17]

The Metropolitan series on social insurance was an impressive effort, probably the most extensive of its day. Monographs appeared on old age dependency, unemployment insurance, health benefit programs, and experience in England and Europe. As revised, the first volume would be used in fifty copies as a textbook by the Social Security Board in 1936. Distribution was widespread, reaching Calvin Coolidge, Governor Franklin D. Roosevelt, and such officials as the head of the Reconstruction Finance Corporation; that it reached and was noticed by President Hoover certainly can be presumed.[18] Governor Roosevelt was told, "It is our hope that the resulting data may eventually be availed of by governors, legislators, industry, labor, and the public, to enable them to determine which, if any, insurance scheme is best adapted to meet local conditions." A Metropolitan vice-president invited Senator Robert Wagner to lunch to discuss how the work could help him "in connection with the bills which you are planning to introduce in Congress."[19] Over two hundred interviews were conducted overseas and "hundreds" in America. The volumes, with accumulated material, were open to the public. May we not say that to whatever extent Herbert Hoover's interest, expressed to President Ecker, stimulated Metropolitan to begin and carry through this project, it may be at least mentioned as a partial accomplishment of the Hoover Administration? (The president's help was acknowledged in each foreword.)

As Hoover was leaving office it would be possible for the research director of Metropolitan to tell a New York State legislative committee that there were by then (December 1, 1932) "no insurance companies today which would advocate any change in the law which would make it permissible for them to experiment with unemployment insurance." Metropolitan had definitely concluded on the basis of two years of study that it "certainly would not now be willing to undertake such an experiment." He warned that a voluntary plan would work if, and only if, both employers and employees were fully committed to such a plan. The British were disillusioned with their solution and turning to charitable relief; they were even talking of moving workers back to the land. Germany was covering only 12 percent of its unemployed. Present American programs were not working.[20] The Metropolitan abandoned a dozen years of effort on behalf of insurance company-based unemployment insurance.

Nearly a decade of Hoover interest in unemployment insurance located in the life insurance industry thus came to naught. The country had not been much interested during the 1920s; articles and books on the subject were rare and tinctured with the socialist convictions of more than a few of the writers. The organized labor bureaucracy was very little interested, when not hostile. The laws of New York State and attitudes of key legislators and bureaucrats (no doubt obsessed with placing all workers on an equal footing) were insurmountable obstacles. The insurance industry was solvent and growing in the decade and really did not have to add risky new policies or oblige the inclinations of a secretary of commerce. Later, the deepening depression made experiments with unemployment insurance possibly dangerous for companies fundamentally entrusted with the life insurance savings of Americans.

OUR DISCUSSION of old age pensions will make more sense if it is understood that in the late 1920s, as now, the options for financing one's security in old age were (a) savings; (b) continued earnings; (c) support by relatives or friends; (d) downright charity by local government or private associations, including institutionalization; (e) one's own life insurance annuities, if any; (f) pension payments from an employer's fund or union fund or, possibly, a fraternal fund (hopefully actuarially based); (g) regular old age payments paid under state or county law, or both, after establishment of need; or (h) in England and part of Europe, for some workers, social insurance payments funded from previous monthly contributions demanded of the individual and his employer by law.

The times were in flux; that is, the numbers of those surviving past sixty-five were increasing, the unity of the family was feeling stress, urbanization and increased cost of construction were reducing the numbers of bedrooms in new houses and apartments, modernizing medical care was having some effect already on need for institutionalization in county homes, and the diet of people was being modified toward somewhat more sensible nutrition (citrus fruits, fresh vegetables, safer milk). The humanitarian agitation of two generations of progressives, radicals, and then liberals was having an appreciable effect on understanding needs. Employers were feeling a greater sense of responsibility toward employees in the age of emerging "welfare capitalism." Considering the report to the New York legislature by a state commission on old age security in 1930, the *New York Times* could say editorially that, in view of some of the differences between this nation and countries overseas, maybe old age pensions did need serious study here, but not because the current crop of aged persons was now in need![21]

We must not get lost in semantics as we reflect on the hesitant growth of what people were calling "old age pensions" in 1929 and later. These would today be called "old age assistance" payments, that is, welfare payments to those qualifying because of need duly established. These were not social insurance payments, made from a fund amassed by sums paid in advance to a government body by employers and employees during working years, as a guarantee of payments later when eligible. The loose term "old age pensions" can thus be a tricky one. We will see in due course that Hoover's principles will straddle this situation in an interesting way, being partly old age pension and partly social and/or industrial insurance payment.[22]

It was in this climate that Herbert Hoover served as a new president, anxious to strike a blow based on firm appraisal of the facts. What cries there were for doing something drastic about old age pensions were either muted in emotionalism, were part of packages to bring radical change to "the system," or were in any case unable to command much of a hearing due to public disinterest born of lack of knowledge and parochialism. The path to change had not yet been paved in the colleges, the media, or the marketplace. There was already vigorous opposition, usually based on inadequate knowledge of facts and opportunities. The National Association of Manufacturers was particularly outspoken. The group was opposed to the adoption of "any general system of public old age pensions by any state, predicated upon a declaration that arrival at a certain age with a minimum amount of property or income constitutes evidence of destitution, and thereby assures a definite monetary income to such individuals."[23]

To concentrate on the Social Security Act of 1935 is to emerge with the illusion that the nation had no programs of aid in earlier years. In fact, in 1929 there were "mothers' pensions" in all but four states; they paid about $30 million that year to some 200,000 children. Here was a building block for Aid to Families with Dependent Children. Ten states and Alaska had old age pensions at the time, and New York and Massachusetts would join them in 1930. Here were antecedents for Old Age Assistance. There were fifty-one workmen's compensation programs, covering 17,000,000 workers. These paid out $150 million in 1929. About 16,000 crippled workers were undergoing rehabilitation at the time. While a quiet debate over unemployment insurance continued, the magnitude of unemployment and uncertainties in corporate finance after 1930 would crush suggested private sector solutions.

To mention these programs is by no means to claim that they were adequate. Nor was there insurance against illness. There was $5.6 billion in private group insurance in effect in American industry, however, and sixty-one trade unions paid $11 million in fiscal 1928 in benefits, chiefly for old age and death benefits.[24] Neither moderns nor contemporaries would find it easy to be impressed by such figures. Said an industrial relations specialist then, "The remedies and relief for economic old age in the United States are yet in an experimental stage. Experience with state old-age relief laws and voluntary industrial pensions is still too fragmentary and too inadequate to warrant judgment in favor of presently prevailing forms. Far more research and study are needed on the extent of old age dependency, on amounts required for relief, and on administrative techniques." He thought "a coordinated system" would ultimately be developed.[25]

The number of persons over sixty-five in 1930 who were partially or wholly dependent was put at two million by a pressure group at the time. Children and relatives were their first resort for help. However, "There are no exact data as to the number of aged dependents in the United States," said Abraham Epstein on behalf of his pressure group. He put the cost of keeping a person over sixty-five in an almshouse at $10.23 a month. There was something of a flurry in 1930 on the subject of old age pensions. A feature article on existing state laws hit the *New York Times* on January 26, for a bill was pending in Congress and bills awaited action in five states; Epstein's American Association for Old Age Security issued some data on January 5, when New York was divided over the bill pending in that state. Governor Roosevelt said he would not sign a bill unless it included provision for contributions to a fund by the future beneficiaries; like others, he was feeling his way. The commission on old age security reported February 17, 1930, suggesting four bills. One debate would be over sixty-five versus seventy as an appropriate cut-off age. Some thought the need for unemployment insurance considerably greater. On April 12 the governor gave his considered views. Proponents were claiming that thirty-four nations had some kind of dependency legislation. Organizations issued bulletins on both sides of the controversy.[26] That year New York would join the minority of states giving state-funded old age pensions, and so would Massachusetts. President Hoover had every right to believe that the states had already preempted the field or were in the process of doing so.

At the same time this activity was gradually moving forward, categories of employees were thinking of themselves as special cases, entitled to rewards from society. Hoover would soon have in his files an article about teachers' pensions which might well have made him uncertain on equities. The truth was in 1930 that major issues concerning pensions were as yet decidedly not settled by society. The bulk of school teachers had the protection of retirement systems at the time. But there was debate over why the pensions were being paid, with opinion growing that they were designed to increase efficiency, possibly by getting older teachers out of the classroom! A new idea being urged was that such pensions should be part of a general old age economic solution. They should be considered deferred pay. Opinions differed on whether early withdrawals should be allowed. What we now call vesting was under active discussion.[27] Whether Hoover or his assistant, French Strother, did anything about all this is doubtful, and letters requesting specific help in getting pensions for professors and for "old Federal officers" were only acknowledged.[28] Ministers were a different matter. In early September, 1929, an inquiry gave Hoover the opportunity to think about the specific retirement problems of ministers. On the seventh he came up with a pithy statement on the entitlement of preachers to consideration in old age by their congregations. The inner man was revealed somewhat when he wrote:

The nature of the work of the ministers of our churches precludes the thought and usually the possibility that they should themselves provide for their old age. The provision of some form of retirement pension is a duty owed them by the congregations and public they have unselfishly served. Experience and actuarial knowledge are needed to avoid practical financial difficulties; but where these have been utilized, the pensioning of ministers should be generously supported.[29]

It would be a man harboring this hypothesis about persons who "serve" who would soon bring to his thinking compassion for the aging part of the general population.

In 1929 old age pension bills were passed by four states, bringing the total nationally to ten. Bills cleared one house of the legislature in seven more. While a Pennsylvania law was found unconstitutional, in New York, as has been seen, the subject would be studied. In California, the law provided an income of $30 a month, with costs divided equally between the state and the county of residence. Said the past president of the California Conference of Social Work, a minister, "The law is reasonably liberal, generous and helpful. . . . The outlook [elsewhere] is hopeful. *Justice for the aged seems to be on the way* (my italics). Since industry does not look after workers in their old age, the counties and states will do it and pay the bill out of public taxes."[30] Here was the view from spring, 1929, before the depression would erode the budgets of those jurisdictions. Many minds would then be changed as to helping state and local governments to finance their welfare programs. Nor was the picture in all ten states as good as that in California, New York, and Wyoming; in the others the old age pension system was optional with the counties, so that in Wisconsin only six counties, with a quarter of the people, participated.

All of this, in any case, was outside the constitutional concern of President Hoover. As a federal official, 1921-1933, he did not have to deal with the problem of state enactment of old age pension legislation. Feeling as he did about the proprieties of staying out of state internal affairs, he seems not to have had anything to say in public on the subject. Moreover, his official papers appear to be largely silent on the matter. Yet he revealed to a visiting confidant in July, 1930, the view that the state old age pensions were in their economic effects poverty-creating instead of—as they purported to be—poverty-alleviating. Contrast this with the firm statement of an intimate, Ray Lyman Wilbur, in 1936 that "Hoover believed in old age pensions. His original belief was that they should be established by the states. After later study, he felt that the subject must extend further than dependence upon the states."[31] In 1938 on various occasions, he pointed out that he and his party had favored the original old age pension programs of the states (he, in California), and he did not oppose federal financial support of them when it came.[32]   My educated guess is that earlier, during the period of growing state legislation in this area, the secretary of commerce favored this approach.   When the pace slowed down during the presidency (and state solvency came into question) he moved toward the idea that action by the life insurance companies was in order.   In any case, he had put together a package of principles he hoped to follow when instituting government old age pensions.   His idea, apparently, was at some point to replace the state pension approach with a truly national program.

Certain concepts were basic to the package put together by the secretary of commerce and president.   There would be no benefits or payments of any kind en route to the established date settled upon for retirement.   The cost of the whole program would be "lessened by forfeiture of all payments by those who died before sixty-five."   Business and industry would help provide these pensions for their employees by purchase of group insurance.[33]

The principles that Hoover felt should control a pension program in the area we now call old age assistance and old age and survivors insurance have great interest, even though they were never put into the form of legislation or revealed to the public at the time.   They were: (1) Private action in savings and insurance policies should be encouraged "by every device."   (2) Pensions should provide a "bare subsistence" in order not to weaken incentives to work and save.   Anything more should come from the individual's own effort.   (3) The size of the pension should be readjusted from time to time "according to the purchasing value of money."   (In modern terms: indexing!)   (4) On eligibility: those in old age still having enough income to pay income tax, that is, "who can look out for themselves," would get no pension.   Those getting pensions from other sources would also not be eligible.   (Ergo: no double-dipping.)   (5) The role of the national government would be to collect agreed percentages from employer, employee, and the self-employed; it would also supplement collections "from the tax income of the government."   (6) Money collected and allocated would be paid out in grants to the states; they would have to "assume part of the load."   (7) The states would have responsibility for administration.   (8) The books on the system would be closed at the end of each year; thus the payout cost would be budgeted for each year and duly appropriated.   "If the income is insufficient during one year, the rate of collections should be increased the next year."[34] There is little point to speculating on whether the Hoover plan would have been modified with time and experience. It was, after all, a pioneering think piece. We cannot know whether the Congress would have insisted on substantial changes. What we have is an alternative plan to what later developed: two competing yet complementary plans that have been amended and modified repeatedly over half a century.

WHEN President Hoover turned from a possible government plan to what might be done in the private sector, he found it far easier to make what for a time seemed to be real progress. His thinking gravitated naturally to the giant life insurance companies of America—with branches and agents nationwide—as he contemplated the possibilities. Often in years past he had paid tribute to this enormous industry. It was in 1932 that an aide told a college student that three quotations summarized his views. First, Hoover had said there was "no single device in our whole economic system which is greater in its importance in safeguarding the welfare of our women and children." Second, he had called it "the first safeguard" for these persons, so that it was one of the foremost economic guardians of the home. The vast capital it represented was a great stabilizing influence on the nation. Third, he had said that private insurance had a "spiritual value." It helped to meet the financial needs of expanding industry, commerce, and education. The fact was that the 54 percent of the people then owning life insurance had an effect on the stability of the entire social order.[35]

In 1929, as in 1921, Hoover turned first to New York Life and then to Metropolitan—with a general appeal to a group of insurance company presidents in between. His cagey approach that summer to an agent of New York Life came immediately to the attention of his old contact Kingsley, who seemed quite unaware that the president had anything in mind but purchase of a personal policy on his life.[36] The next step would prove more meaningful. Coinciding with a meeting of insurance executives in Washington, D.C. (which he did not have time to address), President Hoover invited the eleven-member executive committee of the National Association of Life Underwriters to lunch at the White House on September 26, 1929.[37] At the time, their companies sold conventional annuity policies in which payments made in advance were duly invested by the companies so that a larger sum could be returned in monthly increments at a given age. They were celebrating in

1929 the attainment of the $100 billion mark in their policy face value.

Talk at the luncheon centered on the president's deep concern over the problem of old age pensions and his desire that the life insurance business move into that area. To do so would be to prevent government from further extending its activities into business and would demonstrate that life insurance was keeping up with the times. Hoover greatly impressed his guests with his actuarial and technical knowledge of the life insurance business. He was aware of the actuarial problems of many organizations that had already experimented with old age policies. He hinted that no company at the moment was prepared to write the kind of policy he had in mind.[38]

The response of the life insurance presidents to the Hoover luncheon meeting is hard to ascertain since only Ecker was to be a White House guest or correspondent in the next three and a half years. Hoover does seem to have telephoned some of them, and he may have talked with some of them when traveling. (On this form of interaction the Hoover scholar is helpless; yet the nonrecorded Hoover interaction was voluminous and of the first importance.)

The major result was the beginning of a long exchange of views with Ecker. Wrote Hoover:

> I'm wondering whether it would be too much trouble for you to have your actuaries prepare a table for me indicating what the cost of an old age pension would be, assuming that there are no repayments of any kind except the pension itself—that is, take some basis, say $1200 a year payable in two cases, one at 60 years of age, and another at 70, and tabulate the annual payments the policy holders of different ages must make, say, from 21 onward.

> It would also be of great interest to know what sort of *lump sum* payment would need to be made at 21 and other ages in order to secure such pension. (Hoover's emphasis.)

> If this is to cause any great trouble, please do not bother about it. It is passing through my mind that we might consider applying some such plan to Civil Service employees by which the Government would make half the contribution, the other half to be deducted from wages.[39]

(The reference to Civil Service personnel disappeared from ensuing correspondence at Hoover's end. Nor was it used by Hoover when recalling this activity six years later.[40]) Ecker answered Hoover on October 8, sending comprehensive tables. We have had considerable experience in developing and administering retirement plans for different types of employment, he said. Wrote Hoover, "The tables you sent me are just what I need for further thought."[41]

Any hopes the president might have had for undisturbed contemplation were dashed when Paul F. Clark, president of the Life Underwriters, quickly revealed Hoover's concern "over the Old Age Pension problem" on the first page of the industry's house organ.[42] Now various inquiries began to come to the White House, with acknowledgment by presidential assistants.[43]

Contact with Metropolitan was by no means over. Hoover wrote Ecker on July 25, 1930, that he had heard "indirectly" that the company had worked out a pension policy which it intended to offer to the public. He would like some details! Wouldn't Ecker like to visit the White House? He would and did, on July 31, complete with a memorandum on the old age pension Hoover had in mind. The memorandum noted that the company would find it easier to keep track of policy holders if an annual premium were required, since single or irregular payments would mean the company could not tell whether a person was dead and would therefore have to carry larger reserves on the chance that he was alive.[44]

The accompanying sample had been prepared "as an experiment," it was said, and "the contract was made as simple as we could possibly make it." Then came the bad news: "Frankly, we do not think that either . . . [of the policies] will sell to any great extent." One reason was that the company would not feel like paying an agent anywhere near the standard rate of commission! If he could be getting $50, he would hardly be satisfied with $5. (He would get 30 percent if writing a regular policy.) The company had gone to the trouble just in case a law should be passed analogous to workmen's compensation, except directed at old age; that is, employers would have to provide retirement coverage. "Were such a law in effect the employee could have one of these policies and the employer could pay the single premium at the required age. The employee would take the policy with him if he changed his employment and the new employer could do likewise." While there was a provision permitting "anyone" to pay the premium, this was only "window dressing."[45] Such a response was hardly reassuring.

But back at Metropolitan its longtime specialist on social insurance, Dr. Frankel, was deep in plans for government liaison with private insurance companies to produce a voluntary old age pension system. During the week after Ecker's visit with Hoover, he outlined his hopes to his superior. During their recent meeting Hoover had displayed his interest in "insurance provision for old age," Frankel wrote. Metropolitan should therefore take the initiative, "suggesting legislation under federal or state auspices in favor of an adequate insurance plan, towards which employer and employee shall contribute on a voluntary basis and encouragement should be given to such plans by either the federal or state government by actual contribution of a part of the cost, relief from taxation, or in some way later to be decided upon." He believed "we could secure the heartiest cooperation for such a plan." Frankel concluded, hopefully, "While the plan would be voluntary and permissive, in time it should become fairly universal and accomplish the results now obtained, under the compulsory plans of certain European countries."[46] The idea was interesting, for several of the European countries had neither voluntary nor compulsory plans. No overseas plan by any means covered a nation's total population.

Meanwhile, those around the president knew of his interest in pensions and did not hesitate to reveal the fact to total strangers. When a citizen from Whittier, California, wrote intelligently in August about old age pensions, he was assured by Strother that the president had given "a great deal of study to the problem of provision for old age" and had asked the committee on Recent Social Trends "to make a special and searching investigation of facts and of methods by which this problem can be met." Further, "The President regards this problem as one of the most pressing before the country and is doing everything he can to arrive at a solution which will really serve to meet it and at the same time be in accordance with the soundest economics." To a citizen from Fort Worth, Texas, he disclosed much that was in his superior's mind. He called it highly important that measures to take care of the aged "be properly formulated so that they will spread the cost of this relief in a way to cause the least possible disturbance to the economic structure of the country." It might still be possible "for most of this provision to be done upon private initiative and by state and local authorities." Various plans had been considered. "The President feels strongly that it is a duty of society by some means to solve this problem, so as to remove the fear of old age from the minds of every member of society." He concluded, "It would be unwise for him to commit his mind to a final plan until the experts have finished their investigations, which are still in progress."[47]

As an erroneous idea circulated in early September, 1930, that a commission to study old age insurance and/or pensions would be created, Strother was forced to write letters contradicting the "'misapprehension." In fact, Hoover had "asked the heads of responsible insurance companies to work on the problem of a feasible insurance policy for this purpose," and he had talked with "numerous" people in an effort to arrive at sound conclusions. The president answered an inquiry from a top civil servant, saying hopefully that the companies were "about to offer a policy to the public covering the entire question."[48] Especially to be noticed is the total absence of the reference to pensions limited to the civil service.

Financial aspects of the several annuity plans created by Metropolitan have some interest even now. Bearing in mind the value of the mid-1981 dollar as 18.5 percent of that of 1930, a 1930 pension of $50 per month at sixty-five could come from any of the following lump sum payments (because invested profitably over the years by the companies): paid at twenty-one—$775, at thirty-one—$1,010, at forty-one—$1,500, at fifty-one—$2,450. Yearly payments beginning at twenty-one would come to $39 annually. There is a certain quaintness to a very early idea pursued by Hoover (camouflaged as an interest in purchasing a policy for each of his grandchildren) that parents or relatives might make a lump sum payment at one year of age to take care of the infant in old age. A mere $300 would suffice. His purpose, say Ray Lyman Wilbur and Arthur M. Hyde, was to develop such policies and "at some state" determine what steps the government would need to take to supplement these or to "assist the companies to care for certain groups, especially older citizens whose premiums would naturally be high."[49] Hoover was counting on arousing public interest through publicity; for example, he planned to buy lump sum policies for his grandchildren as soon as the program was in operation. Initially, Christmas of 1929, and then of 1930, was to be the occasion. Said Hoover later, "The cost was so small that it was hoped it would attract many parents to provide an old-age pension for their children in this manner."[50] The official Metropolitan letter on pre-payment for infants (specifically his grandchildren), written December 18, 1930, would not be answered for a month and a half, however, for by then he could see that the country was not up to following his example in such a matter. He thought it best to delay "until some time when you are initiating a campaign when it might be helpful in persuading people to take this sort of insurance." Then he added, "I imagine in the present dull times there is little being accomplished in this direction."[51]

In considering all of this, the observer will bear in mind that annuities were common in American life insurance at the time (but not usually this kind, where there would be no estate value at death before sixty-five, and not the kind where costs would be shared by employer, employee, and perhaps government). Hoover the engineer certainly realized that the insurance industry would have to conduct studies, engage in experiments, and generally be reeducated before it would be ready to take advantage of national legislation—even if passed. In his *Memoirs* he finally judged that it was not something to push through in a deteriorating economic situation, only a year after the stock market collapse.[52]

Meanwhile, essential ingredients would be public desire and acquiescence by company executives and labor representatives. A first step would be to plant ideas in the mind of the general public. So it was that the president instituted a series of meetings with a master publicist, Samuel Crowther, a writer for magazines of large circulation and a book author. His first overnight visit to the White House came on the weekend of October 26-27, 1929; he had already met with French Strother. We do not know any more about the Hoover-Crowther meeting than clues that can be assembled here and there. Crowther says that he and the president "went fully into the thought of having some insurance company actively go forward in the writing of old-age insurance on a business basis, for we agreed that state old age pensions were in their effects poverty creating instead of, as they purported to be, poverty alleviating."[53]

The first publicity payoff came with publication of an article in the *Ladies' Home Journal*, "Insurance for Old Age," with the subtitle, "It Should Be Possible for Every Man to Carry His Income on His Back." The article was described as "an interview with Frederick H. Ecker, President, Metropolitan Life Insurance Company," even though the prose did not mention his name or use any direct quotes—thus universalizing its findings and opening the door to using without attribution Hoover's own reasoning. Its central ideas are similar to the ones in the Hoover *Memoirs*. "Those who die and get nothing decrease the cost to those who live and receive pensions," said the article. Thus the principle was the reverse of fire insurance: there, surviving buildings finance payments for those that burn; here, the pool of those dying before sixty-five finance years of payments to those who live on. "It may be said at once that if we consider an old-age pension as a right accruing to everyone who reaches a certain age, and to be paid by the state regardless of circumstances or consequences, we find ourselves in an impossible situation," for a large liability and substantial increase in taxes would accompany universal pensions. Corporations might be a mechanism for setting aside sums required in the plan, half and half with employees. (Estate value could be had by paying extra.) There would be full vesting regardless of job changes. The amounts paid and received should be commensurate with previous earnings. The plan could be extended to industry in general; the idea was "perfectly feasible."[54] A series of articles in *Forbes*, a magazine read by executives, was a second Crowther effort, in which, as he put it, he said "the same thing in a different way."

Crowther was also involved in an approach scheduled to be arranged with the United States Chamber of Commerce, for Hoover thought its support might well be arranged. By early May, 1930, Crowther had talked with Secretary of Commerce Robert P. Lamont. Crowther's contact with the Chamber was its president, William Butterworth. Overnight stays at the White House continued from May through August, 1930; for a time it looked as though Crowther would be commissioned to write a full-dress book. financed by Metropolitan, based on a major investigation of social insurance overseas. Over dinner Crowther told Hoover and Henry Richard his reasoning:

> I said that I thought a book would have to be written . . . in which the actual experiences abroad would be given at first hand and from an economic and business angle instead of from the social worker's angle and that all our people suffered from a lack of knowledge of the subject—that they were overwhelmed by the emotional appeal to help the aged and that they could only answer "high taxes" and that this was not an answer at all.

Maybe the Chamber would help finance it, Hoover said; in due course he would bring all the parties together.[55]

Crowther then went to New York to meet with Ecker, who drew up some sample policies which struck him as being attractive. But Crowther came to believe that the book idea would not fly, even though "all the information is coming from the several active societies that are advocating pensions" (presumably of the social insurance kind). He did think that "everyone concerned is anxious to work and the only delay has been in making sure that they were working to the best advantage and in the direction that the President most desired." Another meeting with the president ensued.[56]

During the nine months Crowther spent on this project in 1930, he reached the point where he could even telegraph George Akerson, presidential secretary, to please have a car meet him at Pennsylvania Station in Washington as he arrived by train from his Long Island home, "for it rather simplifies getting into the White House."[57] But he became increasingly impatient at the slow progress being made. Through the years other projects would be discussed with the busy and worried president. The White House stays of October 26-27, 1929, May 14-15 and August 11-12, 1930, and September 10-11, 1931, on the pension matter would be augmented by visits March 30-31 and August 11, 1932, and February 1-2, 1933, chiefly on the crime problem.[58]

We cannot detour to describe the efforts of the desperate president late in 1931 to get Ecker and his industry colleagues to purchase mortgages from banks as a way of helping the banks and preventing foreclosures. The idea came to naught as a major factor in ameliorating depression conditions, but there was some cooperation—limited by the crushing burden that policy loans and cash surrenders of policies were having on the cash flow of the companies. While on paper the assets of the companies now came to $16 billion, only $25 million could be pledged to the president's purpose by Metropolitan. Hoover's reply to this essentially negative response to his trial balloon was a bit formal. "I want to thank you for your letter of October 16th and the suggestions it contains. I am glad to have them," he wrote.[59]

So, overall, the Crash, developing into an economic disaster, must be related to the failure of the American life insurance industry to push successfully Herbert Hoover's idea of having the private sector provide old age pension opportunities for the nation's aged and for those looking toward old age. Wrote Hoover in retrospect, "The slump, however, caused the companies to withdraw from this project and await a more favorable moment to launch it." The death of his project was a cause for regret, since it "might have given us great experience and made it possible to reduce the extent of governmental action." That he contemplated legislation that would provide government payments to underwrite the pensions is stated forthrightly: "I had suggested to the companies that if the idea was attractive to the public, we might consider some form of Federal grants to them, as an aid to lowering the cost to the beginners in the older groups whose premiums would necessarily be high."[60] The failure to get the companies started, and the accompanying failure to arouse major public interest, we have to conclude, meant that President Hoover never reached this stage.

SIMULTANEOUSLY with his liaison with the giant insurance companies in the interest of old age pensions, President Hoover was taking another approach designed to educate himself and to influence intellectuals, teachers, and opinion leaders. Reasonably well known even now is the major outgrowth of that effort, the mammoth book, *Recent Social Trends in the United States*, published with great pride by McGraw-Hill on January 2, 1933, with a foreword by the outgoing chief executive. It was the first of fourteen volumes to result from the coordinated research effort of the President's Research Committee on Recent Social Trends (RST) and its investigators. Beginning officially in December, 1929, the effort was, as the scholars would say later, "unique in our history," since "for the first time the head of the Nation has called upon a group of social scientists to sponsor and direct a broad scientific study of the factors of change in modern society."[61] The financing, arranged by Hoover, was by the Rockefeller Foundation; liaison with the White House was shared by presidential assistants French Strother and Edward Eyre Hunt, two intellectuals who displayed both competence and creativity, greatly contributing to the final result.[62]

The genesis of the RST work was a luncheon meeting in the White House attended by Hoover, Strother, and Professor Howard W. Odum, of the University of North Carolina, on April 26, 1929.[63] The first meeting of the social scientists with Hoover was at dinner, September 26, 1929, two days before the luncheon meeting with the insurance company presidents. There can be no doubt, now, that President Hoover anticipated that the work of the scholars on RST would lay the groundwork for some of the social programs he hoped would mark his administration (which at the moment he had every reason to believe would last two terms). It will be seen to be quite incorrect to say that from the outset of his presidency he thought of his second term as the time when he would use this study as an aid to striking a blow for his ideas.

Many clues, as will be seen, reinforce the plain evidence of intention to achieve in the first term. When sociologist William F. Ogburn emerged from a long conversation with Strother in early September, 1929, he declared to a colleague in confidence that while he guessed that neither Hoover nor Strother were yet prepared to tell exactly what it was they wanted, "I gather that [they] know in a general way that Hoover wants to do something in the field of human welfare, such as . . . the family, housing, recreation, or child welfare. . . . And I think that he has in mind the restructuring of the

Department of the Interior, or else the strengthening of it, or the rebuilding of it in such a way as to function largely in this field. I think Hoover has this very much at heart but hasn't given much thought to the details or the means."[64] Ogburn—who would turn out to be the workhorse and the hub of the RST study, exceeding the efforts of Charles Merriam and the others—would meet often with Strother and Hunt, and sometimes with Hoover, during the next three and a half years.

Strother wrote Ogburn in early October, "I know how close to the President's heart this field of inquiry is and how much value its results will have for him in his own efforts to be of practical use in the field of social service." When *Baltimore Sun* journalist Gerald W. Johnson inquired about the project in December, 1929, Strother replied at length. The country, he said, looks to the White House "for inspiration and leadership in social and economic movements for the well-being of people generally." It had become clear to the president that social scientists and welfare workers were groping in the dark for lack of data on the national social structure and statistics. In eighteen to twenty-four months the work would be done (it was not), marking an epoch in such matters. "Such a research has never been undertaken here nor in any other country."[65]

The official White House press release announcing the RST study, December 19, mentioned in its second sentence that subjects to be studied would include "the improvement of national health and vitality, its bearing upon increased number of persons of 'old age' and other results." The goal would be systematic facts about social problems hitherto inaccessible. The *New York Times* carried the RST story on December 20, featuring in its second sentence the idea that the field of study would comprise "the improvement of national health and vitality, its bearing on the number of persons of 'old age,'" and mental and physical health in urban America. The study would be scientific research and would produce systematic facts.[66]

It seems to be relevant that on January 11, 1930, the *New York Times* ran an editorial containing a few comments on the lack of data on old age economic dependency. It quoted Abraham Epstein, of the Association for Old Age Security, as saying that it was a field without exact data and prolific in guesswork. Possibly the president read Epstein's comments when they appeared, or he read the editorial. He certainly did not need a push from either, as we have seen, to be concerned about the aged citizen. But he might have been gratified indeed at the editorial's final sentence: "It would be interesting and instructive to have President Hoover's committee on 'social trends' bring back some fairly definite information on this subject."[67] A few days later Hoover and Hunt spent some time going over the plans for the RST study, especially the schedule for its completion in whole and in part. Told that the appearance of 1930 census data only in 1931 and 1932 would necessitate delay in the final report to as late as February, 1932 (it would be later than that), Hoover showed his great concern and hoped that re-warming census data would not become the focus. It was re-assuring to be told that little more than a third of the topics were dependent on the census, and, as Hunt put it, "later topics dealing with government policy" were independent of such data. According to Hunt, the president then made statements to the effect that "questions like old age pensions were coming up and that action would be necessary. Couldn't this be explored without waiting for Census data? . . . To be of use to him he must have results of the study during his term, remarking that he did not expect to be re-elected." Then, "later he said that results in the summer or autumn of 1932 would be of no use for this purpose"; Hoover said he might be quoted.[68]

The rest of the Hunt-Hoover talk shows convincingly that the president, a man of affairs and of action, hoped that the committee's findings would come to him piece by piece and that he certainly intended to root policy formulation in what came in—not during a remote second term but at once. Immediately on leaving the president, activist Hunt told French Strother that chapters of the study should be placed on an "elastic schedule" so that when finished they would be submitted to Hoover; Hoover in turn would decide whether to release them to the public or hold them for the final report. Meanwhile, recorded Hunt, the president would have "immediate use of them for administrative guidance." Where delayed census material should be involved, "no presidential action can be expected."[69]

Now Hunt would turn to Ogburn with his intelligence. He told the scholar, "The President said that he hoped for some results within one year, and to have influence on adminstration policy he would have to have results about on the schedule originally planned. I stated that it was our understanding that the report was a report to the President and must be of use to him." Howard W. Odum was assured on February 5 by Strother, "At the moment the President has no subject other than the Old Age problem that he would suggest for earlier treatment." Later on, he might.[70] We do not know, as usual, what was said in the numerous face-to-face meetings of these parties or what was conveyed in their long distance calls, but what we do know is that on March 12 two investigators on contract with the RST committee began a special study of old age. The work of P. K. Whelpton and Warren S. Thompson, specialists with the Scripps Foundation for Research in Population Problems, was completed on June 3 and sent to the president on June 14. It contained "such material as could be quickly assembled bearing directly on this timely subject." But the report had already reached White House insiders.[71]   There is no reason to doubt that the report was in fact read by the president, given all of this maneuvering and special action.

The hundred-page manuscript, plus appendix tables, stamped "Strictly Confidential" and bearing the simple title "Old Age" would not be a part of the final *Recent Social Trends* book, nor would it be included as such in the volume the authors would publish later under committee sponsorship. Its first paragraph posed the questions, "To what extent are people able to support themselves when too old to work and how many of them are dependent on relatives, friends, or charity? Are old age pensions necessary, and if so, should they be worked out through private employers or the state?" The final twenty-two pages were devoted to old age pensions of two kinds—those set up by employers and those paid by the states. No consideration was given to annuity schemes of the kind that had occupied Hoover and his friends in the insurance industry (naturally, since the writers were not aware of them). Facts on industrial pensions had been hard to come by: "Because of the recent date at which most industrial pension plans have been established it is not yet generally realized what a given system will cost the company putting it into effect." Most data was from unpublished sources. Fewer than 20 of 300 companies questioned had their plans on an actuarial basis, and only six states and nine large cities had set up pension plans for their employees. But plans for teachers existed in twenty-one states, and all larger cities provided for police and firemen.

Still other information unknown to either experts or the public was absorbed by Hoover. On old age pensions, a survey of industrialists in Pennsylvania found that of 126 replying, 83 favored some form of state pensions financed through public funds. There was a very wide difference of opinion as to what plan to follow

and on what should be done. Some pointed out that to move forward at the state level in this field might put industries in the
state at a severe disadvantage; federal action might be better, they
thought. In any case, the study concluded that improved purchasing power among older people would be essential in the future.
Its practical peroration was: "Charity may continue to be necessary to prevent some older people from starving, but greater opportunity for productive work and continued earnings later in
life together with a more effective method of assuring an income
when work is no longer possible, would make the elders better
customers and would help to maintain a large market of high con-
suming power."[72]

One other advance report, on crime, went to Hoover in September, 1930, but a request for a copy to send a commission on the
subject was refused by the committee; there would be no other
advance services! Feeding confidential data to a public official,
even the president of their nation, offended the sense of academic
propriety of these typical (even though outstanding) academicians.
The RST chairman even had the gall to say in his transmission
letter for "Old Age" that the committee saw itself as "a group of research specialists making a scientific report to you for *public* use.
(My emphasis.) The preparation and dissemination of publicity
describing the report seem to us a proper function of the Committee, and we have prepared summaries to be released later to
the public, outlining the facts found."[73] This could hardly be called
tactful, and behind the scenes there would ensue discussions among
the professors on the propriety of serving a sitting political figure
who would be running for reelection some day. (They were, of
course, privately financed and cherished the idea that they had
themselves gotten the funds through intervention by the Social
Science Research Council, but in fact it was the Hoover pipeline
that worked with the Rockefeller Foundation in the 1920s and
during the presidency that was responsible.[74]) Odum, godfather
to the study and a pioneering researcher in every sense of the
word, scarcely concealed his disgust over the ivory tower attitudes
of the committee. On the eve of the project he blurted out to one
of them, "Witness the senior members of even this committee of
ours and their inability or unwillingness to dig in deep enough to
see the magnitude of the President's proposed research."[75]

It was during these months that a euphoria swept over Hunt,
Strother, and apparently even the president as they considered

what might still be accomplished during the Hoover term despite the Crash. Hunt wrote the *Survey* magazine's editor, Paul Kellogg, that it was "initially hoped" that the RST work would be "the basis for a report with special emphasis on problems which lend themselves to practical solution, their causes and relationships." In reply: "Unless I read the signs all wrong, he [Hoover] has one of the greatest chances in his career. Do underscore it with him."[76]

Surely it is significant in this regard that when Strother found it necessary to retire from office for a time, the president chose to replace him with (otherwise rather surprisingly) the assistant secretary of the New York State Charities Aid Association, George A. Hastings. And finally, in cinching our case that the RST effort was no mere exercise by academicians for academicians (the way it is normally treated), Hunt wrote in June, 1930, "not for printed publication," that the RST Committee was doing research on the underlying facts of American life "that affect the welfare of the people." On its data "all agencies of social welfare may base their projects for social amelioration."[77] Does not the case for practical, timely, and useful research seem quite overwhelming?

Recent Social Trends would turn out to be of first-class importance. It would get unexampled publicity for its vast storehouse of facts.[78] Its influence would be unquestionably major. Yet the study itself failed (except for our one "Old Age" example) to serve the busy and purposeful president of the United States who requested it, because its academic authors were unable or unwilling to put their time into underwriting with hard data any case or cause for immediate legislative enactment. (Times would certainly change in later years, as Rand, System Development Corporation, and other think tanks working at what may be called applied scholarship would do what the campus for so many years would not—and then finally did only with some guilt feelings and frequent recriminations.) The RST Committee would have been shocked had it known of Hoover's private comment in January, 1930, that he did not expect to be reelected and that he counted on the results arriving long before summer, 1932.

Before finishing with old age pensions, we must turn to the Hoover *Memoirs*, with their several pages of clues to his feelings on the subject. These were filtered and possibly modified by two decades of events. He judged, "The organization of old-age assistance under some Federal scheme was an inevitability." More people were living longer, thanks to medical science; the states were preparing their own legislation in the area; the county commissioners' poor house solution was inadequate; and "some part of the people could not, even with thrift, provide for old age; and another part, through shiftlessness, would not." As far as he was concerned, "The height of the world's greatest depression was no time to introduce such ideas [as those he suggested in the cabinet and presidential years], even had we possessed the leisure time to formulate the plans. Our first job was recovery of employment, and any such widespread action was bound to produce some shocks to the economic system." But he did set up a Committee on Social Trends, he says, because he wanted to meet the problem of old age assistance.[79]

WRITING two weeks before the end of the Hoover administration, Strother opined that "a President's paramount influence upon the nation's history is often by way of the ideas which he impresses upon the nation's thought." Good enough. But the impact of those ideas, one might think, should be visible in the immediately succeeding years—certainly within the next decade or so. Yet this may not prove to be the case, especially with ideas which get overwhelmed by dramatic events or which face mindsets so firm that the ideas have little or no chance for a fair hearing.

What are we to conclude as we consider the subject of Hoover and his pension ideas? Not, really, that he had a direct impact on the field of legislation devoted to this subject or on the minds of the experts who would emerge to dominate it. We may conclude, however, that Herbert Hoover did in fact devote thought and time to the thorny question of income maintenance in time of unemployment and old age, relying on private instrumentalities that would be supplemented by government. Further, that he started to set in motion a program to mold men's minds in the direction of implementing those ideas. Then, that he laid the groundwork by commissioning a serious research study by the best scholars in order to create a basis for action in the welfare field.

If one must speculate on what happened to the Hoover plans for private company underwriting of unemployment insurance and old age benefits, 1921 to 1933, the answer is both obvious and obscure. Obvious is the total lack of knowledge of unemployment insurance feasibility in the American insurance industry in the 1920s. There was willingness but no burning desire to take on the New York State legislators, whose laws prohibited experimenting in order to gain experience with policies of a new kind. Obvious also in the light of what has been revealed here is the failure, in general, of the academic social scientists of the Recent Social Trends project to accept the idea that they should leave their ivory towers to give rapid, direct, and perhaps public research help to a sitting president so that he could plan and then, perhaps, design new welfare legislation for the national good.

We have to accept the plausible Hoover evaluation that, due to economic depression, the times by 1931 were no longer ripe for leaders like himself to stimulate the public to insure the old age of children and youth by lump sum payments made decades in advance. But he had also been told that insurance salesmen could not make much money selling old age pension policies of the kind he suggested and thus would be unwilling to sell them. One speculates that the concept of using public funds to underwrite the old age benefits of those unable to pay for them was an original idea so foreign to contemporaries that the president was reluctant even to talk candidly about it with highly placed professionals. (They leaked some of what he did tell them.)

As for extending to America the social insurance of the kind then practiced overseas, Hoover in the fall of 1930 was seeking reliable facts on welfare programs in England and Europe. The extent of planning in the United States—except in the minds of a handful of specialists, planners, and radicals—was totally inadequate in his presidential years as a basis for new public policy. (It would be two and a half years into the Roosevelt administration before a social security act would be passed; the resulting act would be flawed, requiring amendment routinely for decades thereafter simply to achieve rudimentary equity.)

The state old age pension (welfare) activity was spreading in those years, but slowly. Its constitutionality had been successfully challenged in one state. County and state solvency soon became inadequate to the task at hand, especially as the base of aged persons expanded and the financial standing of the work force eroded. At the same time, unfortunately, the ability of individuals to provide for their own well-being—as against unemployment and old age—deteriorated rapidly. Reliable facts on this were hard to come by.

It appears unfair to fault a president under such circumstances for continuing to study and ponder, while waiting impatiently yet hopefully for the facts on which to base policy that would be acceptable to public opinion. Most of his waking hours were in any case devoted to stimulating employment and averting collapse of the economy and with it the American capitalist system.

The nature and dimensions of the Hoover old age pension plans are reasonably clear. There was the idea of new insurance policies that would provide annuity payments in old age. These would normally be paid for by parents in a lump sum or by the individual over the years. Costs might be supplemented by employers. For some, government might help in the financing. Then there was the idea of government old age pensions, with the federal government deducting amounts from paychecks and getting payments from employers (the self-employed also participating); funds would be transferred to the states, who would administer the program in other respects and would probably help finance it.

Compare the above to the old age portion of today's social insurance and public assistance, where there emerged two quite different programs: "social security" and old age assistance. The former is funded from a special tax on employer and employee; the latter is paid from general tax revenues. Funds received from the social security tax go temporarily to trust funds, from which the Treasury may borrow at very low interest, greatly supplementing general revenues from other taxes. Everybody over sixty-five would become eligible for payments from one program or the other, or both at once. There is no estate value other than, at the moment, a death benefit. Because the revenues are not to be invested and do not compound (and for other reasons), the tax has had to be increased regularly. Amounts paid to a person are only partially commensurate with those paid in. The sovereignty of government, its integrity, and national humanitarianism guarantee the system. And the elected and appointed officials of government at three levels usually administer the programs—for better or worse.

IT HAS SEEMED unnecessary to load down this exposition with analysis and conjecture on what these facts have revealed about Herbert Hoover's political economics, that is, his view of the role of the state in society. Various terms are being used in an effort to characterize Hoover's purposes, methods, and goals. My perception is that he believed first and foremost in what we may call "the cooperative state," for "cooperation" was one of his favorite words. He made his devotion to this trait clear on a variety of occasions. Industry, labor, government, and the public should cooperate for the common good without massive legislation or vast restriction by laws or unnecessary administrative controls. The individual was always the key; but some persons, he realized, will always need a helping hand. Voluntary organizations should be given the first chance to help. Then government at some level—and ultimately at the national level—has an obligation of leadership: "a leadership state," one might say. Leaders have inescapable responsibilities—especially leaders with long experience and specialized education. Good will, sacrifice of self-interest, taking the long view, and never straying from fundamentals should serve well the country and the people living in it. Here, in summary, appears to be the philosophy that guided Secretary of Commerce and President Hoover in the years 1921 to 1933, as he engaged in planning and work for the economic security of Americans.

One aspect of Hoover's planning for economic security for the nation's aged must be stressed. He believed, spoke about, and had further plans to encourage preparation by individuals for their own old age through savings and investment in private annuity insurance policies. Social insurance, he thought, even pensions with private companies that might come to be underwritten by government, could not do the whole job. It is noteworthy that in the past decade, despite the existence of social security and public assistance programs for half a century, a major thrust in the United States has been to use tax laws to help create and expand retirement funds in the private sector by individuals themselves. (The tax amendments of 1981 especially furthered this goal.) Hoover would have applauded this long overdue emphasis on self-help during working years to ensure financial happiness during retirement years.

Has all this been worth remembering in the 1980s? Many obscure details, old meetings, speeches long forgotten, and memoranda and letters revealing high hopes, details of conferences in rooms long since refurbished—it all seems so long ago. The book *Recent Social Trends* and its companions had their fundamental impact, no doubt. The insurance leaders were stimulated and encouraged to make their pioneering studies of social insurance; they also had to focus on writing group policies for the nation's industries. A few new annuity policies were developed, but little came of that. The way was paved somewhat for those who later would want to create unemployment insurance, for the secretary of commerce helped to highlight the need, even if his solution was not chosen. A major series of monographs on social insurance at home and abroad, prepared by the largest of the private life insurance companies, was carried through with the distinct encouragement of the president. These would prove useful at the time to authorities in New York State and soon to a federal government pondering social security legislation.

We can now see that America once had before it alternative ways of meeting major human needs. People would come to believe that government programs—not just their own planning, saving, investing, and insuring—are absolutely central to economic sufficiency in old age. Hoover would have deplored this result. Indeed, he did so in later years in speeches and books. He accepted some parts of the Social Security Act as passed while criticizing some provisions. Overall, that piece of legislation was not in philosophy, content, or outcome what he seems to have preferred, but he did not oppose it.

We have seen that the secretary of commerce and president gave thought to the problem of economic dependency among both the unemployed and the aged. It should not have been a surprise to learn that he cared deeply about the social welfare of people at home, just as he did those overseas. The programs he favored for a time cannot be fully judged, for they were never put into effect. Nevertheless, it is quite clear that they were tailored to help preserve the kind of economic and social system he is well known to have favored. That system, in his view, was a partially regulated capitalist system in a country possessing a cooperative government, blessed with intelligent and dedicated leadership, and peopled by families who would want to participate fully in preparing to rise above adversity.

NOTES

1   Herbert Hoover to Darwin P. Kingsley, Nov. 17, 1921, Commerce: Kingsley; Hoover, "Address to Metropolitan Life Insurance Co. Managers Banquet," ms. (Jan. 27, 1923); Hoover to Joseph S. Frelinghuysen, Aug. 15 and 18, 1921, Commerce: Senate; all in Herbert Hoover Presidential Library (hereafter cited as HHPL), West Branch, Ia. An unusual amount of archival assistance was given to the author during the period in which this paper was researched. Thanks are due Tom Thalken, Robert Wood, Dale Mayer, Dwight Miller, Betty Gallagher, Mildred Mather, and Cora Pedersen, archivists at the HHPL; and Charles Palm, archivist at the Hoover Institution.

2   Harley Fiske to Hoover, Aug. 12, 1922, Commerce: Fiske. HHPL. (Hereafter, the reader may assume that cited correspondence and files are in the HHPL, except where otherwise noted.)

3   Hoover to Mitchell, July 29; Mitchell to Hoover, Aug. 3, 1921, in Lucey Mitchell, *Two Lives* (New York, 1953), 364-67; William Starr Myers and Walter H. Newton, *The Hoover Administration: A Documented Narrative* (New York, 1936), 475. Daniel Nelson, *Unemployment Insurance: The American Experience, 1915-1935* (Madison, 1969), covers the general subject.

4   Hoover to Gompers, Oct. 23, 1920, Commerce: Industrial Waste Committee.

5   Marquis James, *The Metropolitan Life* (New York, 1947), 227-28.

6   "Unemployment Insurance," *Transactions of the Actuarial Society of America,* vol. 24, part 1, no. 69 (1923), 1. Lee K. Frankel's and Miles Dawson's *Workingmen's Insurance in Europe* (New York) had been published in 1910.

7   Hoover, "Address to Metropolitan"; Herbert Hoover, *The Memoirs of Herbert Hoover* (3 vols.; New York, 1951-52), II, 102.

8   Hoover to Gompers, Feb. 19, 1923; Fiske to Hoover, April 2, 1924, Commerce: Unemployment.

9   Fiske to Hoover, March 13; Hoover to Fiske, March 29, 1924, Commerce: Unemployment.

10   Copy attached to Fiske to Hoover, March 13, 1924.

11   James, *Metropolitan Life,* 230-31, 432.

12   Edward Eyre Hunt, "Nation Planning," ms. (May, 1931), Hoover Papers, Hoover Institution.

13   Swope to Hoover, June 20, 1930, Presidential: Unemployment.

14   Ecker to Hoover, Feb. 24, 1931, President's Personal File (hereafter cited as PPF).

15   *Ibid.*

16   *Ibid.;* Hoover to Ecker, Feb. 27, 1931, PPF.

17   Exchange of telegrams, March 30, 1931; White House Diary; letters of introduction forwarded to Ecker by letter of April 2, 1931, HHPL. The travelers were Lee K. Frankel, vice-president; James D. Craig, chief actuary; and Rodney Olzendan, research director. The series reached thirteen volumes and appeared during 1931-33, with revisions to 1935.

18   Based on copies of correspondence received from Metropolitan.

19   Frankel to Roosevelt, Dec. 4; to Wagner, Dec. 29, 1930, Metropolitan Life Insurance Co. Archives, New York.

20   Roderic Olzendan, "An alternative to Unemployment Insurance" (Memorandum to the Joint Legislative Committee on Unemployment of the State of New York, Dec. 1, 1932. (This includes Olzendan's own complex plan.) Bornet Collection, HHPL. Photocopies of many of the materials cited here are in the Bornet Collection.

21   *New York Times,* Feb. 21, 1930, p. 18.

22   For a contemporary appraisal, see Glenn A. Bowers, "Economic Old Age: The Public Looks at the Problem," in *Proceedings of the National Conference of Social Work* (1930), 258-65 (hereafter cited as *Proceedings,* 1930).

23   Quoted in Bowers, "Economic Old Age," 287.

24 See John B. Andrews, "Progress of Social Insurance in America," in *Proceedings*, 1930, 258-65.

25 Bowers, "Economic Old Age," 279-82.

26 *New York Times*, Jan. 6, p. 27, April 13, p. 20, June 29, II, 2, 1930.

27 Rainard B. Robbins, "Teachers' Pensions and Our More General Old Age Problem," *Transactions of the Actuarial Society of America*, vol. 31, part 2, no. 84 (1930), 230-44.

28 Chamber of Commerce, Idabel, Okla. to Hoover, Dec. 17, 1929, PPF: Pensions. Such correspondence was common.

29 Hoover to (name withheld), Sept. 7, 1929, PPF: Pensions.

30 Robert E. Lucey, "Industrial Life: Gains and Losses," in *Proceedings of the National Conference of Social Work* (1929), 329-32.

31 Samuel Crowther to Strother, July 24, 1930, Strother Papers. Cf. Ray Lyman Wilbur and Arthur M. Hyde, *The Hoover Policies* (New York, 1937), p. 91.

32 Herbert Hoover, *Further Addresses on the American Road, 1938-1940* (New York, 1940), 13, 33, 35, 40, 55, 56, 62, 68, 73, 202.

33 Hoover, *Memoirs*, II, 313-15; Myers and Newton, *Hoover Administration*, 405. Additional details appear in the *Memoirs* (II, 314), where there is given the text of a memorandum the former president says he circulated to colleagues which spelled out his principles on old age pensions in general. The original memorandum has defied efforts of archivists to locate it, probably because Hoover often loaned important documents in later years and did not always get them back. Discovery of the Crowther files might solve this mystery.

34 Hoover, *Memoirs*, II, 313-15.

35 The quotations are from Hoover to Paul F. Clark, Sept. 28, 1932, all quoted in Strother to Frank O. H. Williams, Nov. 29, 1932, PPF: Insurance.

36 Kingsley to Hoover, July 22, 1929, Presidential: Insurance.

37 White House Diary, Sept. 26, 1929. (The date in the *Memoirs* is incorrect.)

38 Paul F. Clark's account in *National Underwriter*, Oct. 11, 1929. Courtesy Bonnie Chernin, Archives Librarian, Metropolitan Life Insurance Co., who also performed other useful services.

39 Hoover to Ecker, Sept. 28, 1929, Presidential: Pensions.

40 Hoover to Lawrence Richey, Jan. 19, 1935, Post-Presidential: Richey.

41 Ecker to Hoover, Oct. 4; Hoover to Ecker, Oct. 5, 1929, Presidential: Pensions.

42 *National Underwriter*, Oct. 11, 1929.

43 For example, Sun Life Assurance of Canada to Hoover, Oct. 14, 1939, and reply, Presidential: Pensions.

44 Internal memorandum to "Mr. Ecker, President," no signatory. Copy in Strother Papers, 1930.

45 Ecker to Hoover, July 31, 1930, PPF.

46 Frankel to Ecker, Aug. 6, 1930, Metropolitan Archives.

47   Strother to Walter Key, Aug. 21; Strother to W. P. Groves, Sept. 6, 1930, Presidential: Pensions.

48   Strother to Congressman Vincent Carter, Sept. 12, 1930; Hoover to John W. Philp, Sept. 10, 1930, Presidential: Pensions.

49   Wilbur and Hyde, *The Hoover Policies*, 92.   Nineteen eighty-one v. 1930 dollar calculation made by researcher for the Federal Reserve Bank of Cleveland, June, 1981. *Oregonian*, June 27, 1981.

50   Hoover, *Memoirs*, II, 315; Myers and Newton, *Hoover Administration*, 406.

51   Ecker to Hoover, Dec. 18, 1930; Hoover to Ecker, Jan. 27, 1931, PPF.

52   Hoover, *Memoirs*, II, 315.

53   Crowther to Strother, July 24, 1930.

54   Samuel Crowther, "Insurance for Old Age," *Ladies' Home Journal*, March, 1930.

55   Crowther to Strother, July 24, 1930.

56   *Ibid.;* White House Diary, Aug. 13, 1930.

57   Crowther to Akerson, Aug. 9, 1930, Secretary's File.

58   White House Diary, these dates.

59   Ecker to Hoover, Oct. 16; Hoover to Ecker, Oct. 21, 1931, PPF.

60   Hoover, *Memoirs*, II, 315.

61   From the committee's foreword to one of the subsequent books, Warren S. Thompson and P. K. Whelpton, *Population Trends in the United States* (New York, 1933), v.

62   All facts and generalizations in this section rest on the writer's own extensive research on RST, not on two thoughtful accounts with which my narrative differs in at least three important respects. See Barry Karl, *Charles E. Merriam and the Study of Politics* (Chicago, 1974), Ch. 11, and his "Presidential Planning and Social Research: Mr. Hoover's Experts," *Perspectives in American History*, 3 (1969), 347-409. Subject to modification, I believe, are these judgments in the latter: (1) that the committee "was given a three-year mandate"; (2) that "Hoover had planned the whole program as part of a campaign for a second successful administration" (both p. 364); and (3) after a quotation from the committee saying it hoped its work "may prove of value to the American public," the statement that it then "entered into oblivion" (p. 405).

63   White House Diary, April 26, 1929; Odum to Strother, April 18, 1929, Strother Papers.

64   Ogburn to Wesley C. Mitchell, Sept. 6, 1929, Box 13, Ogburn Papers, University of Chicago.

65   Strother to Ogburn, Oct. 4, to Johnson, Dec. 9, 1929, Strother Papers.

66   Press release. Mimeographed. Ogburn Papers; *New York Times*, Dec. 20, 1929, p. 1.

67   *New York Times*, Jan. 11, 1930, p. 16.

68   "Social Trends," Hunt's "Memorandum of a Conversation with President Hoover, January 14, 1930," Hoover papers, Hoover Institution.

69 *Ibid.*

70 Hunt to Ogburn, Jan. 15, 1930, Box 12, Ogburn Papers; Strother to Odum, Feb. 5, 1930, Strother Papers.

71 Mitchell to Hoover, June 14, 1930, Presidential: RST Old Age; Hunt to Strother, May 26, June 6, 1930, Strother Papers.

72 P. K. Whelpton and Warren S. Thompson, "Old Age, A Report Sponsored by the President's Committee on Social Trends," ms. (n.d.), Strother Papers, file "Old Age," 1930.

73 Mitchell to Hoover, June 14, 1930.

74 A typical demonstration of the illusion is in Odum to Hoover, Feb. 9, 1954, Post-Presidential. See also Strother to George E. Vincent (president of the Rockefeller Foundation), Oct. 22, 1929, Ogburn Papers, Box 12; and Vincent to Strother, Oct. 23, 1929, where Vincent says, "The President has talked with Mr. Mason and with me about his plan, so that we have a preliminary familiarity with the purposes of the proposed study. It is needless to say that anything in which the President asks for the cooperation of the Foundation will receive the most careful and sympathetic examination." Also Strother to Ogburn, Oct. 23, 1929. Both in Strother Papers, file "Old Age."

75 Odum to Ogburn, Sept. 30, 1929, Box 13, Ogburn Papers.

76 Hunt to Kellogg, March 1, 1930; Kellogg to Hunt, April 18, 1930, file 627, *Survey* Papers, Social Welfare History Archives Center, University of Minnesota.

77 "Accomplishments of the Administration in the First Sixteen Months," typescript, Hunt Papers, Hoover Institution.

78 A thoroughly researched and documented conclusion I have not yet published; it differs 180 degrees from what is commonly accepted. See how the careful scholar Frank Freidel summarized in 1981 the existing viewpoint of the secondary literature, writing that RST "attracted little attention outside of the scholarly community." "Hoover and Roosevelt in Historical Continuity," in U.S. Congress, House, 96th Cong., 2nd sess., *Herbert Hoover Reassessed* (Washington, D.C., 1981) Senate Document 96-63, p. 281; this may be compared with my contrary judgment there in "An Uncommon President," p. 85, based on my archival investigation.

79 Hoover, *Memoirs*, II, 314-15.

Commentary: The Quest for Security

Joseph F. Wall

THE ADVISORY committee of the Center for the Study of the Recent History of the United States must be commended for its choice of a theme for this year's conference, the third such conference to be held under the Center's auspices. The first meeting, held in 1979 with "Three Iowa Progressives" as its theme, surely evoked nostalgia, perhaps even some despair from its audience, which perforce must gaze out at the current Iowa political landscape decorated by the eminent presences of those three stalwarts of Iowa neo-conservatism, Roger Jepsen, Chuck Grassley, and Terry Branstad. The second conference, in 1980, devoted to "Three Faces of Midwestern Isolationism," was equally archaic in theme. Midwestern isolationism, if indeed it ever really existed, had certainly been lost somewhere between Pearl Harbor and My Lai. The Iowa farmer of 1980, worrying over Russian grain embargoes as he rode down country roads in his Datsun pickup truck, had become as internationally minded as J. P. Morgan ever was.

But for this year, the Center has chosen a theme as contemporary in its relevance to our concerns as today's newspaper headlines. "The Quest for Security," taken in its broadest meaning, would, of course, involve two of present-day America's most sacred cows: national military security and federal social security. Both are sacred to the overwhelming majority of the American people, but unfortunately we are finding it increasingly difficult to place them both on the same altar. The United States is at last having to face up to the painful choice with which poorer nations have long been confronted: Which will it be, guns or butter? For, if I may continue with and mix my metaphor a bit, cows, sacred or otherwise, are not oxen any more in allegory than they are in agriculture. Cows make poor draft animals, as any farm boy could tell you. One cannot yoke them together and have them pull as a team. Given the choice of one sacred cow over the other, it is quite apparent to which cow the non-elective officials of the Reagan administration—the Weinbergers, the Haigs, and the Stockmans—would prefer to give the available hay. To them, the sacred cow of

Joseph F. Wall is Rosenfield Professor of History and Director of the Rosenfield Program in Public Affairs, International Relations and Human Rights, Grinnell College.

social security has become a white elephant. But it is equally certain that the nervous elective Republican officials, even the most hawk-like congressmen, who must face their constitutencies in a general election next year, are determined not to starve social security. So we have the stage set for one of the most interesting political dilemmas to divide a triumphant majority party since 1937, when Franklin Roosevelt confronted another American sacred cow, the United States Supreme Court. The Center could not have chosen a historical theme more timely or controversial than is "The Quest for Security."

The contents of the papers given at this conference, however, give attention to the historic parentage of only one of these sacred cows, federal social security. Both objects of our veneration are, to be sure, of relatively recent conception. A conference devoted to the theme of the quest for security, as related to either of its present major components, would have had little meaning or interest for nineteenth-century America. Along with our seemingly unlimited free land, land that Thomas Jefferson assured us would provide individual economic security for a thousand generations, we also had what C. Vann Woodward has aptly called free military security. Three thousand miles of water on the east, six thousand miles of water on the west, weak neighbors to the north and south all provided us with a God-given moat that made unnecessary a search for security through armaments. As late as 1889, President Benjamin Harrison, after providing a military parade to welcome the delegates to the first Pan-American Conference, could turn to his assembled guests and say with pride, "We have put on this military show for you today not to demonstrate how much but how little military strength we have." Imagine, if you can, any American politician today bragging about America's military unpreparedness. The raucous cries of a few hawks like Admiral Mahan and Teddy Roosevelt in the late nineteenth and early twentieth centuries could safely be ignored in spite of two world wars. We prepared for war only after we got into war, and we dismantled our military machine as soon as we had won that war. The quest for security through militarism did not become a holy mission until 1948, with the onset of the Cold War.

The quest for individual security through some kind of compulsory social insurance system began somewhat earlier than our quest for military security, as the three papers you have heard this afternoon make clear. But even if one accepts the earliest dates suggested by Hace Tishler, Roy Lubove, and others, this second quest for security is still largely a phenomenon of twentieth-century America. And it remained unclear as to what form it would or should take until the actual work of composing the Social Security Act began in 1934, thus predating our commitment to military security by only some fourteen years. Prior to 1900, most certainly, and prior to the onset of the Great Depression in 1930 for most Americans, as Lubove and Clarke Chambers in his paper today state, voluntarism was the only acceptable source of relief for those who through no fault of their own lacked economic security. And the just demands upon voluntary agencies for relief would, in this blessed land of opportunity, be minimal—orphans, war widows with small children, the mentally and, in special instances, the physically handicapped. In general, poverty was due to the failure of the individual, or of the system. Our popular culture, unlike the popular cultures of Europe, Asia, Africa, and Latin America, never recognized poverty as a viable sub-culture, with its own values and artistic expressions, its own particular claims upon the larger society of which it was a part. Neither the poor but admirable woodcutter of the German forest nor the romantic wandering gypsy tinker of the English countryside survived an Atlantic crossing to become the heroic protagonist of our native folk fairy tales. Only within the slave culture of black America, a culture that was largely invisible to white America, did poverty have a recognized and respected status.

In such a milieu, it is hardly surprising that little attention was given in America to the social experimentation of nineteenth-century European governments. Poverty we had, but it remained a matter of individual or, at best, voluntary associational concern throughout most of our history. Not until various historic circumstances brought about what may be called the mass democratization of poverty did the quest for economic security become a national concern. The federal government's belated response to this concern was the Social Security Act of 1935.

Although there was strong opposition to the measure when proposed in Congress, what is interesting is how quickly and completely social security was accepted by both major political parties and by virtually all segments of American society. Just as the Constitution when it first emerged from the Philadelphia convention in 1787 was bitterly opposed and was very nearly rejected by enough states to kill it, but had no opponents left five years after its adoption, so just as quickly did social security become one of our most venerated institutions, beyond the attack of labor, business, or any politician who was not consumed with a death wish.

On the evening of September 30th of this year, a group of distinguished Republicans met in Washington, D.C., to celebrate a historic moment. As the clock struck midnight, marking the beginning of a new day, October 1st, and a new fiscal year, Year I of Our Reagan, the celebrants lifted their glasses high and drank a toast to the death, finally, of the New Deal. But some of the more cautious of those exultant Republicans must surely have sensed that even in this moment of triumph there was something in the air more appropriate to midnight, October 31st, Halloween, than to a bright new October 1st. A most troublesome spirit of the New Deal still roamed the land to haunt them. Social security, if nothing else, still survived, and it alone justified an old New Dealer's answering back in the words of Mark Twain: "The reports of my death are greatly exaggerated." Perhaps the wisest and certainly the least controversial statement that has been made this afternoon is that of Professor Chambers: "Yet of all New Deal programs, it [social security] seems the most secure."

Professor Chambers provides us with the underlying reason for the security that social security itself has enjoyed for the past forty-five years. Social security owes its invulnerability mainly to the political sagacity of its chief architect, Franklin D. Roosevelt. Roosevelt wanted to build social security into the permanent structure of the commonweal, something that could not be repealed by later and less generous Congresses, a program that could not be trimmed out of existence by more parsimonious succeeding chief executives. The only way to achieve this, as Chambers succinctly points out, was to design "a system of social insurance that would be national, compulsory, and contributory, with recipients entitled to benefits as a right, not as a gratuity." In the words of Roosevelt as quoted by Chambers, "We put the payroll deductions there so as to give the contributors a legal, moral and political right to collect their pensions and their unemployment benefits. With those taxes in there, no damn politician can ever scrap my social security program."

And Roosevelt was right. Conservation Corpsmen and CETA workers have come and gone. The government giveth with the left hand to the arts and the humanities, to college students, veterans, and farmers; and it taketh away with the right hand what it giveth. But social security, like Tennyson's brook, goes on forever.

In opting for a contributory system for the financing of social security rather than financing out of general tax revenues, Roosevelt differed with some of the oldest and staunchest supporters of social insurance, who wanted general revenues to be used as a first step toward a meaningful redistribution of income. But for Roosevelt and Frances Perkins, ideology had to yield to pragmatic politics. It was more important to them to secure social security than to reach out for a more all-encompassing but highly elusive social structural change. As a result, many of the radical reformers, as represented by Harry Lurie, and also some of those reformers closer to the center and hence closer to Roosevelt—as Chambers properly emphasizes—were highly critical of the resulting Social Security Act of 1935 and immediately began to work for amending it.

Although Chambers calls Frances Perkins the mother and E. E. Witte the father of the Social Security Act, he appears to agree with Harry Hopkins that the real inspiration for America's social insurance system came not from the pragmatists who wrote the bill but from the more idealistic social reformers who had for thirty years been "in the vanguard of progressive social legislation." Chambers states that "it still remains the case that a coalition of social reformers and social workers, moved by a vision of social justice and social democracy that in no way challenged traditional economic structures or political processes, composed a cadre of concern that played the largest role in preparing for a broad acceptance of a social insurance strategy, in designing the program itself, and in carrying it through to enactment."

Professor William Graebner, in the second paper presented this afternoon, seems to be questioning Professor Chambers's evaluation of the true spiritual godfathers and godmothers of social security, and even its parentage, as ascribed by Chambers, to Perkins and Witte. "Neither Edwin Witte, the titular head of the Committee on Economic Security, nor Arthur Altmeyer, assistant secretary of labor and chairman of the technical board of the CES, had much to do with the drafting—and, I am tempted to say, conceptualization—of the legislation," Graebner tells us. Within the Committee on Economic Security, which created and drafted the Social Security Act, four persons played the key roles in determining what the legislation would look like: Barbara Armstrong, Murray Latimer, J. Douglas Brown, and Otto Richter.

This point of difference between Chambers and Graebner as to which individuals, representing quite different social interests,

are largely responsible for the formulation of the Social Security
Act involves more than a difference between two historians in
their laudable efforts to establish genealogical accuracy. At least
for Graebner, it is essential to the major thesis of his paper that
the inspiration for and formulation of social security come not
from Chambers's "coalition of social reformers and social workers,
moved by a vision of social justice" but rather from tough-minded
lawyers (Armstrong), industrial relations counselors (Latimer), industrial relations economists (Brown), and corporate actuaries
(Richter) who were motivated by visions of greater efficiency and
saw the beneficial impact that social insurance for the elderly
could have upon the labor market, in good times as well as in bad.
Retirement on pension becomes a method of social planning and
control that makes sense to both the social scientist and the more
enlightened business executive. This interpretation sees the Social
Security Act of 1935 not exclusively as an emergency act, created,
as Graebner states it, "to *solve* a dependency crisis,"[1] but rather as
an instrument to *create* dependency for greater efficiency. If I
have any major criticism of Professor Graebner's thesis, it is that
it is too negative in tone, with its emphasis upon dependency. One
can use this same thesis to argue that social security provided not
dependency but rather retirement opportunity (an idea I find increasingly attractive as the years pass) and also greater social
justice within the labor market.

Professor Graebner, to give substance to his interesting thesis,
finds evidence in three twentieth-century precedents: the privately
endowed Carnegie Foundation for the Advancement of Teaching,
created in 1905, the Civil Service Retirement Act of 1920, and the
Railroad Retirement Act of 1934.

The Carnegie Foundation was created ostensibly to provide
pensions for superannuated college teachers. Some years before
he created this foundation, Carnegie had been shocked to learn
how little college professors were being paid, most of them earn-
ing less than he had paid file clerks at Carnegie Steel. Few professors could afford retirement, and few college administrators
were hard-hearted enough to dismiss into destitution aging scholars
who had given forty or more years of distinguished institutional
service. Carnegie, in selecting Henry Pritchett, president of MIT,
to head the foundation, found precisely the right man to carry out
not only Carnegie's desire to help impoverished professors but also
his desire, as Graebner puts it, "to invigorate higher education

with a spirit of enterprise and efficiency." "But," Graebner continues, "Pritchett went beyond Carnegie in his desire to create an organization that would encourage a socially responsible outlook in the professoriate. Carnegie would have been satisfied with mere efficiency; Pritchett sought a kind of control." I cannot entirely agree with Professor Graebner's disclaiming for Carnegie any interest in social control. Carnegie's interests were somewhat different from those of Pritchett, but both sought to use the lure of pensions to control higher education. Pritchett sought to introduce standards for admission into institutions of higher education and thereby force the upgrading of secondary education. Carnegie sought to secularize private colleges and universities by denying his pension plan to any college that had religious requirements for its students, faculty, or trustees.[2] Carnegie was using his great wealth to force secular humanism. He is not one of the Moral Majority's great heroes.

This point of issue that I raise regarding Carnegie's Foundation for the Advancement of Teaching is a minor one, however, and to the extent that it is germane to this discussion, it but further strengthens Professor Graebner's thesis. Carnegie's actions, like those of Pritchett, are illustrative of the power of pensions to create, through dependency, desired social control.

I find Graebner's thesis persuasive not only in his use of the three antecedents to social security, but in his interpretation of the formulation of the Social Security Act itself. As he tells us, his argument rests upon three forms of evidence: the "direct" evidence as contained in the testimony given before the CES and in the oral history memoirs of Armstrong and Brown; the "indirect" evidence of the larger historical context within which social security was created; and finally, the "logical" evidence, that is, the relationship between social insurance and labor force participation rates. Curiously enough, I find this last form of evidence the most convincing of all. As is often true in criminal cases, so here too circumstantial evidence can be more persuasive—and certainly easier to come by—than the "smoking gun" itself. But, as I am sure Professor Graebner would agree, to say that social security was *intended* to have a labor market impact does not preclude other purposes that the many authors and enactors of the bill had in mind.

One of the many values that Professor Chambers's excellent paper has, particularly for the non-expert in the field, like me, is to provide the reader with a brief but comprehensive historio-graphical survey of the literature on social insurance. His dis-cussion of the recent revisionist interpretation of the origins of the social insurance system in the United States as presented by Edward Berkowitz and Kim McQuaid provided me with an insight for more fully understanding Professor Bornet's impressively long article presented this afternoon.

In commenting upon Professor Bornet's paper, I should first like to consider it on its own merit, and then relate it to the two papers that preceded it. Bornet tells us in his introduction that his "interest in social welfare goes back a quarter of a century," and his "research on Hoover longer than that." It has obviously been a labor of love. At the Center's conference of two years ago, Richard Lowitt commented upon what he called "the rehabilitation of Herbert Hoover now under way." Lowitt believes that "Scholars, who, more than ever before, are showing an increased interest in ideology, now find Hoover a provocative and exciting figure."[3] It is an interesting phenomenon in revisionist history, even though there appears to be some danger that we might go beyond re-vision into meta-vision in our efforts to rehabilitate the thirty-first presi-dent of the United States. Professor Bornet can not only claim membership in this school of history, he may properly be called one of the founders.

Bornet's stated purpose for this essay was to piece together a story "about the desires, hopes, and plans of Secretary of Commerce and President Hoover in the area the public has come to call social welfare. . . . For Hoover did in fact leave a record of dreams and efforts in this humanitarian area, just as he did in so many others." No one can fault Professor Bornet for not fulfilling this expressed thesis. In meticulous detail, he gives us a full account of Hoover's interest in developing a social insurance system, including efforts in the last desperate summer of Hoover's presidency to achieve some kind of national insurance plan, working through the private sector but encouraged and supplemented where absolutely neces-sary by the federal government. The research that Bornet has undertaken in this largely unexplored area of Hoover's career is exhaustive and impressive. It is also, for this reader at least, a study of frustration and failure.

I find something pathetically naive in the picture that Bornet gives us of Hoover's making plans in the winter of 1930 to estab-lish a $300 annuity fund for each of his grandchildren to set an example for other Americans, showing them how they could plan ahead for the financial security of their descendants. He was contemplating this as the nation was plunging into the Great Depression and millions of Americans were worried about the current month's rent, not retirement for their grandchildren.

Hoover's program of establishing voluntary group annuity plans to provide security for the elderly was, of course, not an original idea with him. The first group annuity plan was established in the United States as early as 1921. But while other forms of group insurance, including life and health, increased rapidly during the 1920s, group annuity lagged far behind for the simple reason that the major life insurance companies had discovered that they lost money on such plans. The few companies that offered group annuity, such as Aetna, Metropolitan, and Connecticut General, did so as a kind of loss leader to induce large clients to buy their far more profitable health and accident group plans. As late as 1938, when Bankers Life of Des Moines first began to consider entering the group insurance field, its chief actuary, Dennis Warters, discreetly made inquiry, among his fellow actuaries in the major insurance companies which issued group plans, as to the profitability of group insurance. All of his friends told him the same thing: group life was highly profitable, as was group accident and health insurance. Group hospitalization was very questionable, and group annuities were actually sold at a loss.[4] This may well explain why Hoover did not get a warm reception from New York Life and Metropolitan for his scheme of a national pension plan that would be compatible with his basic ideology.

Although Professor Bornet has provided me with all of the details that I needed to know as to *what* Hoover's planning for social insurance was, I am not satisfied with the *whys* as given in his paper. What motivated Hoover to push so steadily and persistently in this field throughout the 1920s and early 1930s? Bornet seems to be satisfied with attributing this to Hoover's humanitarian impulses. But I find this an incomplete answer. For example, Bornet quotes Samuel Crowther as reporting in 1930 that Hoover opposed the few existing state old age pension plans as being "poverty creating instead of, as they purported to be, poverty alleviating." Yet Bornet, on "an educated guess," sides with Ray Lyman Wilbur, who said Hoover actually favored state pension plans. There is nothing, apparently, in Hoover's papers that would indicate conclusively which was Hoover's true position. His own proposals, however, would strongly suggest that he would reject governmental pension plans in favor of social insurance provided through the private sector. If humanitarianism were the compelling motive for Hoover to push social insurance, then it would seem that he would be more receptive to proposals for government financed plans.

Viewed from the perspective of Berkowitz and McQuaid, however, Hoover's motivation for the plans he actually proposed is clear. And if one borrows Professor Graebner's thesis and applies it to Hoover, then one can find a motivation that is quite consistent with Hoover's ideology. Neither Pritchett nor Carnegie would have any difficulty understanding the whys of Hoover's proposals. He, like them, sought greater efficiency through the social control that private pension plans provided.

The history of social insurance in this country is rich with paradox, as these three papers have shown: enlightened business men giving their early support to social insurance at the same time that labor leaders were resisting the idea; idealistic social reformers urging the financing of social security from general welfare revenue funds at the same time that progressive New Deal officials sought a special and essentially regressive tax. Nothing in social security's history, however, is more paradoxical in light of what was eventually to result from social security than the fact that the leadership of the Republican party in 1934-35 fiercely fought the Social Security Act. As it turned out, social security has enabled many thousands of elderly people to leave their homes in the Middle West and the Northeast to seek a new place for themselves in the sun. Roosevelt, ironically, through social security did more for the Republican party of Arizona; Orange County, California; and Dade County, Florida, than he ever did for New York's Tammany Hall or the Cook County Democratic machine. Social security has geographically concentrated old age and has given it conservative political clout, for the voting percentage of people over fifty is much more impressive than it is for those under twenty-five.

If there is any historic justice, next January 30, 1982, the centennial of FDR's birth, President Reagan should personally unveil that long-awaited Roosevelt monument in Washington. I even have a design already sketched out for it. There will be an impressive marble statue of Roosevelt, seated at his desk and in the process of signing the Social Security Act of 1935. Standing behind him will be the figure of Herbert Hoover, with one hand holding his nose and with the other hand gingerly patting FDR on the head. On the base of this monument will be the inscription:

TO FRANKLIN DELANO ROOSEVELT, FATHER OF SOCIAL SECURITY
ERECTED ON THE CENTENNIAL OF HIS
BIRTH BY A GRATEFUL REPUBLICAN PARTY

NOTES

1 Emphasis added.

2 Joseph Frazier Wall, *Andrew Carnegie* (New York, 1970), 870-80.

3 Richard Lowitt, "Commentary," in John N. Schacht, ed., *Three Progressives from Iowa: Gilbert N. Haugen, Herbert C. Hoover, Henry A. Wallace* (Iowa City, 1980), 54-55.

4 Joseph Frazier Wall, *Policies and People: The First Hundred Years of Bankers Life* (Englewood Cliffs, N.J., 1979), 102.

Social Security: New Directions

Rita Ricardo-Campbell

THE SOCIAL SECURITY program as an entity is politically irreversible. Even though it must be changed to ensure its long-run financial integrity, the word on Capitol Hill is that "there are no Medals of Honor to be won on this one." That the social security program is regarded as politically irreversible when considered as a unit does not mean that any change in future benefits should be automatically ruled out. An immediate reduction in the existing railroad retirement benefits, already integrated with the social security benefits, was enacted only one week ago, September 28, 1981. It was explained that "this legislation was considered essential to the solvency of the [railroad retirement] system. . . . Without these amendments, we'd be facing a cash-flow crisis in 1982 or 1983."[1] Thus, quietly, the smaller railroad retirement program (about one million beneficiaries) was cut and its payroll taxes raised while Congress ducked the predicted 1982 shortfall in the Old-Age and Survivors Insurance (OASI) trust fund, with its over thirty million beneficiaries.

Many academicians, legislators, and others concerned with public policy formulation would like to strip the social security benefits of all welfare-type components. Their proposals attempt to relate benefits to the taxes paid in an individual equity manner, as private pensions relate premiums to benefits. I believe that this is impossible to accomplish because of specific technical difficulties and the political climate. However, the proposal has great appeal because it concentrates welfare benefits on the truly needy rather than diluting the amounts among all the aged.

If the welfare-type benefits were eliminated from the social security system, it would in effect require tremendous expansion of the already existing welfare program: Supplemental Security Income, or SSI, established in 1974. Its means-tested benefits are supported entirely by general revenues and are awarded on the basis of proven need.

In each year since 1974, the OASI trust fund has paid out more in benefits than it has received in tax revenues and interest payments. There is an immediate need in October, 1981, for additional

---

Rita Ricardo-Campbell, Ph.D., is Senior Fellow, Hoover Institution, Stanford University.

revenues to meet the promised retired-worker, spouse, and other benefits that are paid from the OASI trust fund. If inflation continues, slowing down increases in the total of social security benefits alone will not prevent the anticipated exhaustion of the OASI trust fund during the latter part of 1982. A one percent increase in the cost of living means a $1.3 billion increase in the amount of benefits paid. Infusion of monies from the separate Disability Insurance trust fund will only slightly delay a negative balance. Use of the Medicare, Part A, Hospitalization Insurance trust fund monies—all three trust funds are part of social security—may give a year or two of grace. However, inpatient hospital costs during the first quarter of 1981 rose at an annual rate of 18.3 percent over 1980, and deregulation is anticipated to be inflationary.

The 1981 *Trustees' Report* on the Hospitalization Insurance trust fund concludes:

> The present financing schedule for the hospital insurance program is not adequate to provide for the expenditures anticipated over the entire 25-year valuation period if the assumptions underlying the estimates are realized. Tax rates currently specified in the law (including the scheduled increases in 1981, 1985, and 1986) are sufficient, along with interest earnings, to support program expenditures over the next 8 to 10 years. The financing for the remainder of the 25-year valuation period is not sufficient to provide for projected benefits and administrative expenses.[2]

Obviously, the merging of the three trust funds is not the most desirable solution to the immediate shortfall in the OASI trust funds. It would create, earlier than already predicted, a sizable imbalance in the Medicare, Part A, Hospitalization Insurance trust fund and not solve the underlying problems.

Social security benefits, running about $140 billion annually, absorb over one-fifth of the United States budget. Thirty-six million people, more than one of every seven, receive a monthly social security benefit check. Twenty-four million of the thirty-six million beneficiaries are sixty-five years or over, and of these, nineteen million are retired workers. Nearly three million are disabled workers under sixty-five years. Nearly one-half of those receiving a social security benefit are getting benefits that are not akin to annuities or pensions. Social security benefits, unlike private pension benefits, rise with the cost of living. No one receiving benefits today has paid for them in an actuarial sense. These facts make it difficult to compare social security with private pension plans. Yet such comparisons are often made, not only in the popular press but also in the academic literature.

The public perceives the present situation requires drastic changes, new directions: the elimination of some of the program's welfare components. Past federal administrations have hidden the festering financial imbalance behind an unbelievably intricate set of regulations, and they have obfuscated the issues by using inappropriate terminology. The *Social Security Bulletin's* tabulations are still headed by "contribution" for tax, "trust fund" for pay-as-you-go contingency fund, and "premium income" for receipts to the Medicare (Part B, Medical Insurance) "trust fund." Indeed, the heading "premium income" stands side by side with the heading "transfers from general revenues." The latter, in 1980, amounted to $7 billion, as oppposed to only $3 billion of the so-called "premium income." It is no wonder that the public continues to be confused as to who is paying for what.

What can be done? In order to clarify the answer to this question, it is helpful to delineate three approximate time periods: (1) the immediate financial crunch, 1982 through about 1986; (2) a period of financial balance, from about 1990 to about 2005; and (3) a long-run period of financial imbalance which will begin around 2005 and run approximately through 2055, beyond which date the trustees' projections do not go.

It is because of the intervening period of apparent financial safety that economists who are accustomed to looking into the future are concerned. If nothing is done now to preserve the long-run financial integrity of the system, within a relatively short period a new, more serious insufficiency of funds will ensue. Because of the politically dominant social adequacy rationale for the benefits, any changes in the anticipated level and structure of benefits must be phased in over a period of years. If nothing is done, the tax-paying younger workers' faith in their future benefits will deteriorate further. It is more responsible to integrate remedies for the immediate and the long-run imbalances than to consider each separately, even though the causes may differ.

The 1980s imbalance is in large measure due to unanticipated inflation that has pushed up the cost-of-living-indexed benefits while unemployment has been shrinking the payroll tax base from which the revenues come. The use of a cost-of-living index that has heavy weights for housing prices and interest rates to measure the changes in the cost of living of older persons is being questioned. Both housing prices and interest rates have had substantial increases, but they do not necessarily act to diminish the real purchasing power of most older consumers. Persons over sixty-five are less likely than younger persons to buy a home and are more likely to lend money than to borrow it.

A cause of the immediate and the long-run projected imbalance is that the level of benefits has been increased dramatically. In the past ten years alone, average benefits have increased in constant dollars by about 35 percent, while average weekly real earnings of workers in private, nonagricultural employment have declined slightly from 1970 to 1980 and are still falling. The increasing life expectancy and the steadily declining fertility rate since 1958 are the major causes of the long-run imbalance. Whereas in 1960 there were about 5.0 workers for each social security beneficiary, today there are about 3.3, and by 2050 there will be only 2.0 workers to support each beneficiary. Immigration, legal and illegal, may mitigate the decline in the ratio of workers to beneficiaries slightly, but revolutionary advances in biology, such as medical cures from recombinant DNA techniques, would, through extending life expectancy, more than offset any immigration-induced reversal of the aging of the U.S. population. The low birth rates of the 1960s continue into the 1980s. In 1981, there are fewer than 1.8 children being born per woman over her lifetime.

Are young people willing to work and pay increasingly high taxes today on their first dollar of earnings to support the non-taxed benefits that go primarily to non-working, older persons, many of whom have higher incomes and more assets than do the young heads of households? Will young people continue to believe the implied social contract: that because they are paying taxes to support the current aged, their children will accept what may be a substantially increasing tax load to support them, the "between generation." The appropriate level of benefits at any time when real income per capita is shrinking—a new situation in the United States—involves value judgments and needs public discussion.

Nearly 20 million retired workers with 3 million spouses sixty-two years and over, 4.4 million widows and widowers sixty years and older, and only about 15 thousand aged parents of retired workers received social security benefits in 1981. Even a quick look at these data points to the confusion that the Social Security Administration's artificial benefit classifications create.

According to these data, there are 20 million retired workers and a total of fewer than 8 million "spouses." What is not explained is that a spouse, who may be male or female, who paid in social security taxes and is eligible upon retirement for one-half or more of the spouse's primary benefits, may be classified in the benefit tables under "retired worker." The heading "spouse" is a statistical aberration because it includes only those married persons who are not entitled to their own earned benefit in an amount equal to one-half or more of the spouse's retirement benefit. All others are classified "retired workers." This is not mere nit-picking. The resulting confusion can affect national policy. For example:

The 1981 legislative proposal to eliminate the minimum benefit occurred in part because of confusion about who the "dually entitled" are. Many thought that these individuals are federal government employees who are dually entitled to a federal civil service retirement benefit and a social security benefit. They are not. Dually entitled individuals within the social security system are almost all married women who have worked and who receive the higher of their own benefit or a secondary benefit equal to about one-half of the primary benefit of their husbands. A large number of these women, about 800,000, receive the minimum benefit. In order to maintain the illusion that working married women always receive a benefit based on *their* earnings, that benefit is computed first. If it is less than the $122 minimum, it is increased to $122. In the many cases where the wife is dually entitled, this is done by using part of the secondary benefit based on her husband's earnings.

The issue of whether to eliminate the minimum benefit is closely linked to social security's non-coverage of government employees. Many of the higher-paid government workers hope to forestall legislation which would require them to pay the sizable social security taxes, nearly $2,000 annually at the maximum, that almost all other workers must pay. Of the 3,000,000 individuals receiving the minimum benefit, 360,000 are federal, state, and local government annuitants. Federal government workers will be even more opposed to the integration of the civil service and social security systems after the cutback of the integrated railroad retirement benefits.

The happiest solution to the immediate social security financial crunch would be a further decline in the inflation rate and a substantial increase in covered employment. I do not anticipate that these two trends can occur quickly enough and in sufficient degree to eliminate the anticipated deficits during the 1980s in the OASI trust fund. I therefore reiterate the various proposals that I have made in congressional testimony and in the editorial pages of *The Wall Street Journal* and other newspapers.

One way to help resolve the financial imbalance of the 1980s is to implement early mandatory coverage of all federal government workers as a first step toward coverage of *all* workers. Equity demands that there no longer be tax favoritism for selected workers.

Federal government employees have a pension plan, as do most full-time employees of private industry. Unlike most employees of private business, however, their benefits are indexed. Moreover, the government does not merely match one dollar for each dollar of the federal employee's contribution. The employee and the employing agency each pay 7 percent of the payroll that "together constitute 26.5 percent to the Civil Service Retirement (CSR) trust fund income. . . . In 1980, the CSR system's cost to the government was $9.6 billion (65.3 percent of outlays), and over the coming five decades, it is projected to grow in 1980 dollars to $20.2 billion (78.0 percent of outlays)."[3]

The Congressional Budget Office report from which the above data comes points to the generosity of both the benefits and the early entitlement age, fifty-five years, as in part being offsets to the relatively higher pay for comparable jobs in the private sector. The unfortunate outcome of a personnel policy that pays high-level employees, 55-65 years, more upon retirement than if they continue to work is detrimental to the current operations of the federal government.

Women federal employees as a group would benefit from social security coverage because, whereas under the civil service the level of benefits is directly proportional to earnings, under social security there are heavy weights used to compute retirement benefits that favor lifetime, low-earning workers. In April, 1978, 28 percent of federal women employees had annual earnings below $10,000, while only 7 percent of men employees were in these low income brackets. Similarly, minority employees, who are concentrated in the lower civil service grades, would, as a group, also benefit.

For reasons of equity, responsible personnel administration, and the impending imbalance in the OASI trust fund, social security coverage of all federal employees, preferably by integrating the two plans, should be enacted. In mid-1979, three-fourths of men who were receiving a civil service retirement benefit were already receiving a social security benefit or would receive one upon reaching age sixty-two.

Mandatory coverage of *all* federal government employees—2.7 million, effective January, 1982—would yield about $10 billion that year and increasingly higher amounts each successive year.

Short-run disbursements resulting from their coverage would increase only slightly. The long-run, seventy-five years' average savings would be about 0.5 percent of payroll.[4]

There are various options in integrating the CSR and social security systems. The two trust funds would not be intermingled, although their benefits would be integrated, as are many private pension benefits. A gradual phase-in of offsets of the CSR benefit amount against the social security primary benefit or vice versa should be expected. Transitional options include: cover federal employees below only fifty-five years, or fifty years, or even forty-five years. Coverage of state and local employees should follow as soon as the legal problems can be resolved.

To consider the elimination of the minimum benefit of $122 per month to be a substitute for coverage of government workers is illusory. Among the one million civil service annuitants (and an unknown number of state and local employees) who receive more than the minimum social security benefit are many whose average lifetime earnings in a secondary job under social security are low because of the intermittent nature of their covered secondary jobs. Earnings from their primary, civil service job are neither taxed nor counted for benefits. Earners retiring at age sixty-five with low average lifetime *covered* monthly earnings receive tax-free social security benefits that are about 94 percent (if married with entitled spouse) and 63 percent (if single) of their prior years' earnings. High earners receive about 52 percent and 35 percent, respectively. Low average earners obviously have a windfall gain even when their average covered lifetime earnings under social security count for benefits above the minimum.

My second recommendation, one that I believe is politically viable, is to index the monthly social security benefits by the lower of the changes in the consumer price index *or* a suitable wage index. This would help during the 1980s and over the long run. During 1980, social security benefits went up 14.3 percent while wage rates increased 8 to 9 percent. Those years in which real wages fall are historically unusual, influenced by atypical events. It appears unfair that beneficiaries in atypical periods are better protected against price increases than are workers. The history of the United States indicates that in most years real wages and productivity rise. If this proposal had been applicable, it would have saved about $7 billion in the year beginning July, 1980, and several billion dollars in the subsequent fiscal year.

To my mind, this approach is preferable to construction of a special cost-of-living index for older persons. The January, 1981, issue of the *Social Security Bulletin* has an article that attempts to do this. The article states in a footnote that "home ownership is not treated very satisfactorily . . . in the three indices discussed" and that "improving the treatment of home ownership . . . is outside the scope of this article."[5] Development and use of a special index for the aged would deteriorate into a technical discussion about which index is best and why.

My third recommendation is to make it actuarially disadvantageous for persons to retire at ages sixty-two and sixty-three. This proposal ties in with my major recommendation to help solve the long-run imbalance. In early 1981, I developed the details of a gradual phase-in to the full benefit at age sixty-seven which makes it increasingly disadvantageous to retire earlier. Over the next twenty years, the proportion of full benefits paid at age sixty-two would be reduced from 80 percent of the full benefit to 70 percent in 1984, 65 percent in 1988, and 60 percent by the year 2000. Proportions of the full benefit by 2000 would be: at age sixty-three, 70 percent; at age sixty-four, 80 percent; at age sixty-five, 90 percent; at age sixty-six, 95 percent; and at age sixty-seven, 100 percent.

The advantage of discouraging, but not eliminating, the social security benefit for persons under sixty-five years is that it still leaves in the hands of individuals a choice, although at somewhat lower rates than is presently the case. Other economists would gradually eliminate receipt of any benefit paid to individuals under age sixty-five and permit a full benefit at age sixty-eight.

My plan would not affect anyone until 1984, and then only very slightly those individuals who, in 1981, are younger than sixty. A three-year planning period is short, but then the size of the financial imbalance in the OASI trust fund, 1982-86, will be large. This plan does not affect, until 1995, anyone who is planning to retire at age sixty-five. These persons are under fifty-one years of age in 1981. Although one particular age cohort is more adversely affected than others, this has been true throughout the program's history. Among current beneficiaries, no one has paid—in an actuarial sense—for his benefits, while those in the *much* younger age cohorts are paying, especially if they are not married, more than the actuarial equivalent.

The plan recognizes the three years longer life expectancy at birth since social security was enacted in the 1930s. If the 100 percent benefit is set at age sixty-eight, as recommended by other economists, those who have forty years of covered work should be entitled to a full benefit at age sixty-seven. This recognizes that high school graduates enter the labor force and pay social security taxes four years earlier than college graduates, and six or more years earlier than professionals.

But even enactment of universal coverage, indexing benefits by the lower of the rise in the cost-of-living index or the wage index, and gradually phasing in entitlement to a 100 percent benefit at age sixty-seven will not ensure the long-run financial integrity of the social security system. With luck—that is, less inflation and higher employment—the system might balance if the intermediate assumptions of the fund's trustees are realized. But the intermediate assumptions can be questioned.

The difficulty in making estimates for seventy-five years into the future as well as in making the wide range of the existing estimates cannot be stressed enough. The 1981 intermediate "B" deficit of the OASDI combined trust funds (which includes the disability trust fund, the discussion of which cannot be undertaken here) is estimated to average 1.82 percent of covered payroll over the next seventy-five years, and my three recommendations in total do not save this amount.

After the publication of the 1981 *Trustees' Report*,[6] actuary Geoffrey Calvert and I made what we believe are more probable demographic and economic assumptions upon which to base the long-term, seventy-five-year cost and benefit projections.[7] We do not hesitate to point out that any estimates seventy-five years into the future, including ours, are subject to error.

The fertility rate assumed by the trustees is 2.1 births per woman by 2005 and during the following fifty-year period. Our comparable assumption is 1.85 births over the same period. Because of the over two-hundred-year downward trend in the birth rate, increasingly effective and often irreversible birth control methods, and the substantial increase in the number of two-earner couples, many of whom prefer a lifestyle without children, I question the feasibility of the trustees' basic assumption, to which the cost estimates are very sensitive.

The mortality rate has since 1900 been falling at 1.2 percent annually. The trustees' intermediate assumption is that the average annual reduction in the mortality rate will reach one-half of the 1900-1978 average rate by 2005 and be stable at that level for the ensuing fifty-year period. We are more optimistic. Bearing in mind DNA recombinant and other research potential, we believe that the upward trend in longevity will continue and that three-quarters of the 1900-1978 average annual reduction in the mortality rate is a more reasonable assumption than is one-half.

The trustees' long-term projections assume 3 to 4 percent annual inflation, a 1.5 to 2.0 percent annual gain in productivity, and 5 percent unemployment. We estimate 5 percent inflation, a 1 percent productivity gain, and 6 percent unemployment.

If the disability trust fund is included, the trustees' two intermediate estimates of a long-run deficit over the seventy-five years—expressed as a percentage of payroll—are 0.93 and 1.82 percent, while ours is as high as 4.19 percent. Although deficits are probable during the first twenty-five years, it is in the last twenty-five years of the seventy-five-year period that the system can no longer be rescued unless major changes have been made many years before that time. The purpose of this exercise is not to frighten people but rather to point out the extreme sensitivity of seventy-five-year estimates to relatively small and reasonable changes in the underlying assumptions, and the need for action now.

Even though I believe that it is not politically viable in the 1980s to attempt to legislate more than I have already recommended, I am still supporting my recommendations of 1974-75, made when I was a member of the Quadrennial Advisory Council on Social Security. These recommendations would reduce the welfare component in the benefits but would not eliminate it. I propose: over a thirty-year period, a phaseout of the retired spouse's secondary benefit, now one-half of the primary; over a fifty-year period, a phaseout of the surviving spouse's secondary benefit, now 100 percent of the primary; and additionally, for women, earnings credit given for children born. This is a total package that speaks to the increasing burden of the welfare-type benefit payments while there is a growing general revenues-supported welfare system, Supplemental Security Income (SSI).

My plan also recognizes the major socioeconomic changes of the last thirty years: the revolutionary increase in the number of women who work and pay social security taxes, the decline in the marriage rate, and the increase in the divorce rate. For example, in March, 1981, 69 percent of women 20-24 years and 65 percent of women 25-54 years were working. Data for 1979 that includes summer and Christmas seasonal workers shows the following percentages of women having worked during that year: 79 percent of women 20-24 years; 74 percent of women 25-34 years; and 68 percent of women 35-54 years. Although the rate of increase in the number of working women will slow during the 1980s, most women's primary retirement benefit thirty years hence will exceed one-half their spouses' benefit. This is already true for a very large proportion of married women.

There is a danger that the 1977 amendments, by enacting only ten years of marriage prior to a divorce as sufficient for entitlement to a surviving spouse's benefit at age sixty, may eventually break the bank. A divorced spouse's benefit is not counted under the 175 percent of the primary, family maximum limit. Already there are instances where three spouses' benefits, each at 100 percent of the primary, are being paid on a single primary. Although an individual may collect only one social security benefit, this gives many individuals the option of choosing the highest benefit among several, and the load on the higher primaries will increase.

There are many other proposals in addition to those I have already discussed. The most popular in Washington, D.C., is to permit inter-fund borrowing among the three major trust funds. This is potentially dangerous because, since it does not do anything about the basic problems, it will hasten the overall use of general revenues for non-means-tested benefits and will act to anchor, as Medicare, Part A, funds are exhausted, general revenue-supported national health insurance.

Proposals to modify the cost-of-living formula to index benefits with inflation are numerous and varied. One senator has proposed to cap the increases at three percentage points below the consumer price index increases, which would, according to the Senate Budget Committee, save $46 billion in 1982-86. This proposal is not politically viable in my opinion, but it does emphasize how much inflation contributes to the problem.

Among other proposals that I have not discussed are the Reagan administration's proposal to change the complicated benefit formula and its proposal for multiple changes in the disability program. There are legislative proposals to raise further the increasing social security taxes. An interesting proposal by Senator Danforth is to increase taxes on cigarettes and alcohol, and to earmark the revenues for Medicare. There is also the perennial general revenue-funding proposal, which I oppose.

The public is not aware of the amount of taxes they now pay or the level of their benefits in relation to their taxes. A mid-July CBS-*New York Times* poll found that only *2 percent* of the population queried knew that "a person about to retire this summer has contributed to the social security fund in his working career, if he's always paid the maximum social security tax, less than $30,000."

Another 2 percent of the population in the same poll thought that such a person had paid in more than $100,000. Eighty-five percent did not even attempt to place such payments in a dollar bracket.

There is no one receiving social security today who has paid in taxes the full actuarial value of his anticipated benefits. Yet it is over forty years since the system was first started. It is time to destroy the myth that people have paid for their benefits and to restructure the system so that the current and future generations have assurance that they will receive benefits correlated with the taxes they have paid, and are paying.

NOTES

1 "Railroad Benefits to be Cut," *Peninsula Times Tribune*, Sept. 29, 1981, p. D-3.

2 "Annual Report of the Board of Trustees of the Federal Hospital Insurance Fund," mimeographed (1981), p. 40.

3 U.S. Congressional Budget Office, *Civil Service Retirement: Financing and Costs* (Washington, D.C., 1981), p. x.

4 "Report of the Universal Social Security Coverage Study Group, The Desirability and Feasibility of Social Security Coverage for Employees of Federal, State, and Local Governments and Private, Non-Profit Organizations," mimeographed (1980), pp. 47, 49.

5 Benjamin Bridges, Jr., and Michael D. Packard, "Price and Income Changes for the Elderly," *Social Security Bulletin*, 44 (Jan 1981), 7n.

6 "Annual Report of the Board of Trustees of the Federal Old-Age and Survivors Insurance and Disability Insurance Trust Funds," mimeographed (1981).

7 Geoffrey N. Calvert, "The Social Security System: Long-Term Outlook, What Really Lies Ahead?" (New York: Alexander & Alexander Services, Inc., 1981), [3].

4271103

Southern Methodist Univ.   br
HD 7125.Q47 1982
The Quest for security :

3   2177   00963   8154

WITHDRAWN